SOUTH-EAST LAI

CU00822119

Standing alone, as from a rampart's edge,
I overlooked the bed of Windermere,
Like a vast river, stretching in the sun.
With exhultation, at my feet I saw
Lake, islands, promontories, gleaming bays,
A universe of Nature's fairest forms...

William Wordsworth, *The Prelude*

South-East Lakeland

W R Mitchell & Bob Swallow

First published in 1997 by
Smith Settle Ltd
Ilkley Road
Otley
West Yorkshire
LS21 3JP

ISBN 1 85825 077 3

British Library Cataloguing-in-Publication data:
A catalogue record for this book is available from the British Library.

Set in Monotype Ehrhardt

Designed, printed and bound by
SMITH SETTLE
Ilkley Road, Otley, West Yorkshire LS21 3JP

For the dedicated staff of the Cumbria Wildlife Trust

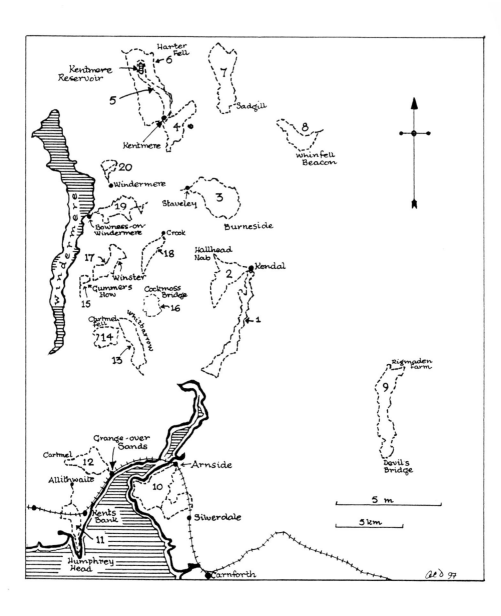

Harter
Fell
←6

Kentmere
Reservoir

7

5

Sadgill

Kentmere

4

8

Whinfell
Beacon

20

●Windermere

19

Staveley

3

Bowness-on-
Windermere

●Crook

Burneside

17

18

Hallhead
Nab

Kendal

Winster

2

Gummers
How

Cockmoss
Bridge

15

16

Cartmel
Fell

Whitbarrow

14

←1

13

Rigmaden
Farm

9

Grange-over
Sands

Cartmel

12

Arnside

Allithwaite

10

Devil's
Bridge

Kents
Bank

Silverdale

11

5 m

Humphrey
Head

Carnforth

5 km

ad 97

CONTENTS

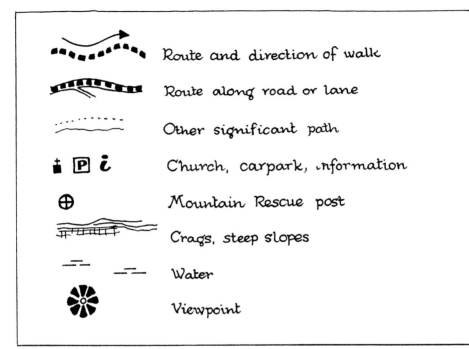

	Route and direction of walk
	Route along road or lane
	Other significant path
⊕ ℙ 𝒾	Church, carpark, information
⊕	Mountain Rescue post
	Crags, steep slopes
	Water
	Viewpoint

Key to Maps

INTRODUCTION

The *Walker's Guides*, devised by Smith Settle, contain much more than basic suggestions for worthwhile outings and details of the precise route. Their special value lies in the back-up provided by notes on landscape, history and wildlife. The walker is informed about sights, sounds and sensations, also the rich heritage of the selected area.

The first book in the Lakeland series guides dealt with Central Lakeland, with its craggy volcanic fells, glacier-hewn valleys and lakes. It is also the district where the spirit of romantic poets, notably William Wordsworth (a great fellwalker), still broods. This second volume, on South-East Lakeland, based on Kendal, includes the high fells of the Kentmere area but deals with more gentle terrain — the Silurian landscape of rolling hills capped by rocky knolls; of deciduous woods, rivers and one notable lake — Windermere — the largest in England. Carboniferous limestone forms a number of fine hills overlooking Morecambe Bay and the Kent Estuary. Here, too, are old meadows and woodlands, little touched by man in recent times, and notable for their diverse range of wildlife and flowering plants.

The walks hinge on the old town of Kendal, gateway to the Lake District, built of the native limestone and sustained during its early growth by the woollen trade. A countryside which at first consideration seems ordinary, as compared with the grandeur of the Volcanics, is found to have many unexpected pleasures. The south-eastern hills have not (yet) been loved to death. Around Grange-over-Sands, the Lakeland Riviera, are fine walks beloved by the Victorian visitors of old, who started walking in almost tropical lushness, with pampas grass and palm trees, and reached an airy summit offering a view of several counties.

The Arnside/Silverdale area, between the A6 and the coast, has been designated an Area of Outstanding Natural Beauty. Woodland walking, in former coppice woods, offers views of deer and squirrels (some of them of the old English red variety). In autumn, a fungal foray offers a glimpse of species with delightful names — elf cups, fairy clubs and bird's nest fungus.

Morecambe Bay and the Kent Estuary, which are overlooked from several of the walks, are a prime area for wintering ducks and waders. Few people could stand unmoved on a limestone cliff-top overlooking the Kent Estuary as the flow-tide begins with a wall of water several feet high and, in ten minutes, a desert of sand and mud becomes an arm of the sea.

The Sands of Morecambe Bay is a general name for 120 square miles (310km²) of sand, mudbar and marsh, which are exposed at low tide. It is then that cross-bay walks are organised under the supervision of Cedric Robinson, guide to the Kent Sands. William Wordsworth wrote that the cross-bay walk was not a deed of derring-do but distinct proof of good taste: 'The Stranger, from the moment he sets his foot on those Sands, seems to leave the turmoil and traffic of the world behind him...' It was the wilderness experience before attaining the promised land of the Lake District.

Walks in the vicinity of Bowness and Windermere were so well used by old-time tourists that they were provided with stone seats. Vantage points were mentioned in the guidebooks, along with a detailed account of what might be seen in clear weather. From Biskey Howe, a walker sees a storm tracking down Great Langdale and, when it has cleared, becomes aware of the rock turrets of the Pikes, blue-grey in the mid-distance. The primary feature is

Windermere, over ten miles (16km) long, which has its head among the mountains and its comet-like tail within a few miles of Morecambe Bay. Hampsfell Hospice, close to Grange-over-Sands, offers an exceptional panoramic view, from Black Combe to Ingleborough.

This book has introductory chapters, followed by notes on twenty well-recommended walks, ranging in length from one mile (1.5km) — to Gummers How — to twelve miles (19km). The notes are attended by sketch maps on which the route of each walk is clearly marked. North is always at the top of these maps.

It is recommended that you carry the appropriate Ordnance Survey 1:25,000 Outdoor Leisure Map (2½ inches to the mile). The English Lakes (South-East) sheet is enough for many of the walks, but the following Pathfinder maps are also required to ensure complete coverage:

Walk	Title	Map No	Name
1	Kendal to Levens Bridge	627	SD48/58 Milnthorpe
9	Updale from Kirkby Lonsdale	628	SD67/68 Kirkby Lonsdale
10	Arnside & Silverdale	636	SD37/47 Grange-over-Sands
11	Allithwaite & Humphrey Head	636	SD37/47 Grange-over-Sands
12	Grange, Cartmel & Hampsfell	636	SD37/47 Grange-over-Sands
13	Whitbarrow & Witherslack	627	SD48/58 Milnthorpe
14	Bluebell Woods & Winster Valley	627	SD48/58 Milnthorpe
15	Gummers How	626	SD28/38 Broughton-in-Furness
16	Down Damson Dene	627	SD48/58 Milnthorpe

On the higher ground, you are free to roam. Some of our walks use paths which have just evolved but are not classifiable as public. Otherwise, the routes selected use public or permissive paths and bridleways. Follow the Country Code.

Thanks are extended to Ruth Pollitt, who provided the paintings and drawings of birds and beasts; to Christine Denmead, who drew the clear and informative maps; to John Bennington, John Morrison, Ron Scholes, Kenneth Shepherd and Barry Stacey, who provided some of the photographs; and to Mark Whitley, whose help, encouragement and comments made the compilation of this guide enjoyable.

W R Mitchell and Bob Swallow, 1997

ACKNOWLEDGEMENTS

Thanks are due to the following people for permission to reproduce the undermentioned illustrations:

John Bennington, pp2, 10, 51, 55; John Morrison, p94; Ruth Pollitt, pp17, 18, 20, 27, 30, 37, 40, 54, 76, 79, 98, 102, 107, 111, 115; Ron Scholes, pp1, 7, 11, 13; Kenneth Shepherd, p117; Barry Stacey, 'Lightwork', front cover, pp50, 71, 74, 95.

All other photographs were provided by the authors.

PUBLIC TRANSPORT

Rail service: North West Regional Railways operate a regular service between Oxenholme and Windermere. There are intermediate stations at Kendal, Burneside and Staveley. The journey time over the whole route is between twenty and twenty-five minutes. Certain trains run through direct from Manchester Airport via Manchester Piccadilly, Bolton, Wigan, Preston and Lancaster. Oxenholme is the junction with the West Coast main line, though not all the Intercity trains stop here. The Lancaster-Barrow service is useful for walks in the Arnside and Grange areas, there being stations at Silverdale, Arnside, Grange-over-Sands and Cark and Cartmel. For timetable and fares, telephone 0345 484950.

Buses: Stagecoach Cumberland buses operate a network of services in this area. Services 518, 530, 531, 535, 730 and 735 operate between Barrow and Ambleside via Newby Bridge, Cartmel, Grange and Kendal. 530 and 531 cover Kendal to Ambleside, but without doubt the most useful is route 555 Lakes link offering a roughly hourly service, Monday to Saturday, between Lancaster and Keswick. The vehicles used are invariably coach type double-deckers, from which there is a splendid view. The Sunday service is much reduced, operating (in January 1997) only between Kendal and Keswick. Telephone 01946 63222 for more details.

TOURIST INFORMATION CENTRES

South Lakeland Tourist Information offices sited within the area covered by this book can be found at:

Bowness, Bowness Bay	015394 42895
Grange-over-Sands, Main Street	015395 34026
Kendal, Town Hall, Highgate	01539 725758
Kirkby Lonsdale, 24 Main Street	015242 71437
Windermere, Victoria Street	015394 46499

The Lake District National Park Authority also provide a wealth of information on the area, their main visitor centre being at Brockhole, Windermere (015394 46601), with a seasonal office at Glebe Road, Bowness Bay (015394 42895).

Fellside, Kendal.

ROCKS AND THE LANDSCAPE

The geology of the Lake District is complex and rich in detail, and the non-specialist is thankful for the neat summaries of perceptive students, going back to the early part of last century, when Jonathan Otley of Keswick, an amateur geologist, defined three main types of rock — Skiddaw Slates, Borrowdale Volcanics and the Silurian Slates. He wrote about them in the *Lonsdale Magazine* and elaborated on the theme in his guidebook of 1823. Adam Sedgwick, a native of Dent who became the Woodwardian Professor of Geology at Cambridge, in a stimulating contribution to Wordsworth's *Guide to the Lakes*, described the effect of each type of rock on the Lakeland landscape.

The Skiddaw Slates, in the north, are not really slates but in the main some coarse-grain flagstones, shales and mudstones which were laid down in a sea basin between 500 and 550 million years ago. This type of material weathers easily. The eroded fragments form scree slopes in the steeper areas. Skiddaw Slates are the stuff of Skiddaw itself, of course, and also brooding giants Robinson and Grasmoor. Visually, the Slates peter out around Derwentwater, but there is a strangely isolated slab, Black Combe, in the south-west.

Slightly younger are the hard, upjutting Borrowdale Volcanics, which as their name

The smooth fells of the great Silurian belt in the Kentmere Valley, which is tucked away from a busy road bypassing Staveley.

I

During the million-year-long glacial period, huge masses of ice ground out the bottoms of river valleys such as Longsleddale, and converted their water-cut V-shape to a distinctive U-shape. Scattered about the valley bottom are moraines, formed from heaps of rubble left by the retreating glacier.

implies had a baptism of fire with the flaring of the Borrowdale volcano. The Volcanics give the heart of Lakeland its dark grandeur, the substances having a wide variety, from lavas like cinders to fine-grain rock like the green slate, a consequence of intense heat or pressure, which was mined at Coniston. An exposure of particularly fine, hard volcanic rock high on Pike o' Stickle, in Great Langdale, was the basis of the axe-making industry of Neolithic times. The Volcanics extend southwards to Coniston and the head of Windermere, and at the southerly margin is a thin and impure band of younger rock known as the Coniston Limestone.

In South-East Lakeland, the dominant feature is the younger bluey-grey strata of the Silurian series, evident in an area from about Windermere to Cartmel. The fells are mainly rounded and have been fancifully compared with sleeping elephants. Such rocks had their origin some 400 million years ago as sediments in the delta of a great river flowing from the north. Referred to generally as Silurian Slates, the terrain consists of various assemblages of rock — grits, flags, shales, slates.

In the course of time, they were folded, as can be seen in quarries and cuttings made for new roads, such as the M6 at the Lune Gorge (*visited at the start of walk 8*). Weather-resistant gritstone is responsible for Gummers How, the highest point, at over 1,000 feet/300m (*walk 15*), but generally these Silurian hills have an elevation of about 800 feet (250m). Rocky knolls form great vantage points and are a joy to visit,

Haweswater from Harter Fell (walk 7). In recent times, two natural lakes were converted by Manchester into a substantial reservoir, displacing in the process the old community of Mardale.

3

Limestone formed from the remains of billions of tiny prehistoric creatures was then uplifted by geological action around 350 million years ago. Subsequent exposure to wind, rain and frost stripped away the thin soil covering and created the grooves known as 'grykes'. Examples of limestone hills in this region include Scout Scar, Hampsfell (pictured) and Whitbarrow, the latter having the largest limestone 'pavement' in Lakeland.

especially School Knott above Bowness (*walk 19*). 'Knoll country' is seen by anyone who uses the B5284, between Kendal and Bowness (*walk 18*). A Silurian Way Trail has been laid out in Grizedale Forest, near Hawkshead.

Kendal's 'auld grey' appearance is derived from a belt of limestone, but notice, as you look at the hills round about, the old Silurian forms (*walk 2*). Rocks of the Silurian period lie cheek-by-jowl with Carboniferous limestone in the little valleys of Winster (*walk 17*) and the Eea, the last-named river draining the Cartmel peninsula. The Silurian rocks are to the west and limestone obtrudes to the east. Limestone forming hills such as Scout Scar, Whitbarrow and Hampsfell was laid down as

sediment, mainly the remains of miniscule and ancient creatures, in a clear, deep sea. The limestone was uplifted by geological changes which occurred about 350 million years ago. It lies mainly horizontally and it therefore does not take much effort to explore it.

Whitbarrow Scar (*walk 13*) is made up of several different layers of Carboniferous limestone. On the surface are the Urswick limestone, outcropping as scarps and areas of pavement on the eastern side of the Hervey Nature Reserve, and Park limestones, forming ridges and hollows to the west. Among the fossils to be found here are brachiopods. The South Lakeland District Council promoted the Limestone Walk, around thirteen miles (21km) long, taking

4

in Arnside, the open mosses between Hale and Holme, and the fells of Clawthorpe and Hutton Roof. A leaflet is available.

What nature gave, nature was to take away. In the restless evolution of the landscape over millions of years, a comparatively recent event now known as the Ice Age was to have a most profound effect. In the Tertiary era, the drainage pattern of the Lake District had been radial. Rivers flowed in all directions from a central dome. Those of the Windermere area are lined up north to south. Some major landscape-shaping came with glaciation. Lakeland was the playground of glaciers, with the ice advancing and retreating on at least three occasions. The periods in between, known as inter-glacials, were relatively warm.

When glaciation was intense, almost all the mountains would be overwelmed by snow, and a build-up led to the formation of ice. A mass of slurring ice plucked out corries and, advancing down the main valleys as glaciers, picked up rocks and other material to form a geological mush we call boulder clay. The glacier, like a gigantic file, deepened and smoothed the sides of old river valleys. Evidence from the bed of Windermere suggests that two glaciers occupied this major valley, each 'river of ice' gouging out a basin in what is now a deep lake.

Look on the knolls of the hills around Windermere for the striations caused by the passing ice. Such scratches proved useful when geologists came to plot the course taken by the Pleistocene ice, which in the south of the district progressed to Morecambe Bay, an area which then (it is assumed) was full of pack ice from the Irish Sea. There would be so much seaborne ice that glaciation would be retarded and further changes inflicted on the landscape.

The final retreat of the ice occurred some 13,000 years ago. The visible Silurian rocks had been smoothed and rounded by

The many knolls around Windermere, such as this to the east of Bowness visited on walk 19, are excellent vantage points from which to view the lake, with its head reaching into the peaks of Central Lakeland, and its outlet over ten miles (16km) away.

5

the ice, though less evidently than with the Volcanics. Lumps of iceborne Silurian rock, named 'erratics', came to rest over a wide area to the south, most prominently on Hampsfell, near Grange (*walk 12*).

Windermere was a much larger lake than now, extending further north. The evidence is in the shape of former islands, now tree-covered knolls about Ambleside. Lakes occupied smaller valleys where now there might be the odd tarn, though the valley bottoms are of peaty material overlying glacial drift. Drumlins, which are rounded hillocks formed of fine glacial deposits, are common on the lower ground between Windermere and Ambleside, and also in the valleys of Winster (*walk 19*) and Gilpin.

As for the limestone, scratching by glacial ice is evident, but in the main the changes have been wrought by thousands of years of exposure to wind, rain and frost, especially rain, which has a weak solution of acid, picked up from the atmosphere and soils, creating grooves in limestone which are called runnels and, when deep, grykes. Notice such features on the summits of Whitbarrow (*walk 13*) and Hampsfell (*walk 12*).

The valleys hold alluvial deposits, eroded from the high hills. At the coastal strip and Lyth Valley (*walk 16*), a depth of over 200 feet (60m) of material with a marine origin has been studied. In Kentmere (*walks 4, 5 & 6*), the mere was reduced in size in modern times, being drained for land reclamation and later dredged to recover diatomite, the siliceous fossil remains of microscopic organisms. The non-inflammable properties are used in the manufacture of boards on behalf of the building trade.

When the scenery was being formed, copper and lead were among the minerals locked in the fells. Quality slate was available in large quantities. Exploiting this natural wealth was to provide the basis of some profitable commercial ventures.

*Snow is not uncommon in this part of Lakeland, and routes such as the Ill Bell Ridge (*walk 6*) — seen here from Hart Crag — are a challenge to the experienced and well-equipped winter walker.*

The weather   Wide variations are experienced in an area which includes high fells and sheltered coastal areas. Grange-over-Sands (*walk 12*) is especially well favoured, being sheltered from the northerly wind and open to the mild west and south-westerlies. Spring and autumn are the driest and brightest times of the year. Summer in high fell country is usually cool and cloudy. Snow may lie on the fells for several months. There may be a covering in late autumn, but the big snows (such as 1947 and 1963) have come well after Christmas. On the northern shore of Morecambe Bay, it is not often — a day or two in the year — that snow lies. The Windermere area has from 50 to 60 night frosts in the year, as compared with about 30 by the sea. The high fell rainfall may exceed 100 inches (250cm) in the year, as compared with about 40 inches (102cm) at the coast. There are therefore days of high humidity.

6

MAN AND THE LANDSCAPE

Some 5,000 years ago, Neolithic (New Stone Age) settlers arrived on the coast of what is now Cumbria. Inquisitive groups who penetrated into the central areas would doubtless find that lakeborne travel in a simple boat such as a dug-out tree trunk was preferable to forcing a way through an almost continuous forest of oak and elm, with pine at higher levels. The early settlers were hunters. The culinary jackpot would be capturing a red deer, which apart from being a huge source of protein, yielded antlers and bones for domestic use, and skins with which to make simple tents. Axe heads and arrowheads of this period have been picked up on High Wray, not far from what is now Windermere station (*walk 20*).

Early settlers would dabble in farming, using the age-old slash-and-burn technique to clear land. The systematic felling of large forest trees was aided from an early date by axes with heads made from an especially fine, hard volcanic tuff wrenched from a vein high on Pike o' Stickle at the head of Great Langdale. A few cattle were kept. The diet would be varied by fish and eels taken from rivers and lakes.

For a thousand years, the settlers left few traces. Then, around 3,000 years ago, the use of bronze spread from the south. Bronze objects have been found in the Troutbeck Valley. An excavation of a Bronze Age burial urn by W G Collingwood indicated that, at this early period, wool was being woven into cloth, of a type which kept the living warm and swaddled

For nearly three centuries the Romans tried to impose order on the wild Cumbrian landscape, constructing settlements and building up military and trade routes. One such high-level route traversed the High Street range, linking Ambleside to Brougham. It was probably an ancient trackway which the Romans improved; there are occasionally faint traces of the original Roman agger or embankment.

the dead. Favourable weather conditions encouraged settlement on higher ground. When, some 2,700 years ago, the climatic pattern changed, with more rain and lower temperatures, the hills proved untenable. The Iron Age, which followed the age of bronze, evolved belatedly in a remote area like Lakeland. The native Celts, stocky, dark-haired folk, were pressurised by the Romans in a northward sweep through Britain in AD 78. Over-running Lakeland, the Romans advanced beyond Solway to establish a defensive line between Clyde and Forth, subsequently falling back to a line between Bowness-on-Solway and the Tyne. The vaunted Hadrian's Wall defined the extent of the Roman Empire and theoretically kept out the Picts. South of the wall and its defensive forts lay a military zone, controlled from yet more forts, each holding a cohort of 5-600 hundred men and connected with each other by good roads. Troops were able to move swiftly to maintain law and order. One suspects that the lives of most Celtic families went on pretty well as before. They kept sheep. The Romans admired their skill at weaving wool.

The legionary fortresses of Chester and York were connected to Lakeland by arterial roads, that from Chester running north to Watercrook, just south of Kendal, thence to Brougham and Carlisle. The main road from York crossed Stainmore on its way to Carlisle. A branch road from the Chester-Carlisle left Watercrook, crossed Trout Beck to Ambleside and met up with a road extending westwards from Brougham, via High Street at over 2,000 feet (610m), thence to the coast at Ravenglass, via the high passes of Wrynose and Hardknott.

Roman control was relinquished after 250 years. Now the lives of the Celtic folk were disrupted from north and west by the Picts and Scots. The Celts fused into a large kingdom known as Rheged. 'Cumbria', used for the modern administrative area, is a revival of an old title signifying 'land of the Welsh'. Few traces of the nature worshipping Celts are to be found in the Lake District beyond the names of some mountains and rivers. The Celtic river names include a clutch in the south — Kent, Leven, Crayke and Winster. Germanic tribesmen, crossing the North Sea to the Humber and moving northwards, created the kingdom of Northumbria. These Angles (the first English) pushed westwards, crossing the Pennines at the gaps of Stainmore and the Tyne. Anglian placenames, with the elements -ham and -ton, are fairly common to the south but virtually absent from the more central areas. The lakes were usually referred to by the Old English term 'mere' or 'water'. Anglian names for features of the landscape include the hill Loughrigg and a promontory called Bulness, now much better known as Bowness.

At the beginning of the tenth century, Norsefolk, popularly known as the Vikings, arrived in western Lakeland as part of a spectacular expansion which was to take others from Scandinavia to the heart of Europe and fog-shrouded, chilly Iceland and Greenland. The Norse reputation for rape, pillage and murder is possibly an effect of monastic propaganda, for the incomers would find the wealthy abbeys a soft target. At Lindisfarne, the monks evacuated their abbey in AD 875 as raiders in longboats swept in from the sea. The monks took with them the uncorrupt body of Saint Cuthbert and the head of Oswald, wandering through the North for seven years before finding a safe home for the holy relics in what is now County Durham. The nomadic monks are said to have lingered for a while in Kentmere, where the parish church is dedicated to Cuthbert (*walks 4, 5 & 6*).

The Norse influence remains strong in the Lake District. The names Vinand's lake (Windermere) and Thurston (Coniston Water) relate to important stretches of water. Lots of -thwaites are found, signifying places where Norse folk cleared land for their settlements. Examples in the south-west are Birthwaite (to become Windermere, a boom town of the railway period), Heathwaite and Finsthwaite. Oats were cultivated at Haverthwaite, in the valley of the Leven, and Grassgarth, near Ings, is derived from the Norse *garth* or *gard*, a small farm. A Norse family had its winter-house in the valley (henceforth known as dale). In summer, the valley land was rested and allowed to grow grass to be wind- and sun-dried into hay, fodder for the stock in winter. Meanwhile, that stock (cattle, sheep, goats) was driven to a *saeter* (grazing ground) on the fell, to take advantage of the summer flush of grass.

Sadgill, at the head of Longsleddale, which means the long valley (*walk 6*), is a curious name to us but simply means 'shieling by a ravine'. The *shieling* was a hut, with facilities for making cheese and thus conserving the goodness of summer milk in a durable form, for use in winter. Ambleside and Hawkshead developed from Norse *saeters*. Satterthwaite and Latterbarrow are names which hint at their old-time use for summering stock. Norse names — now rendered as gill, beck, tarn, force, holme and many others — pepper the map of the Lake District. Trout Beck was first mentioned in 1292 as Trutebyk, and Orrest Head is from an Old Norse word meaning 'battle'.

The Norsefolk transformed the landscape, which became open grassland. As the woodland waned, ling and bracken became conspicuous features of the drier tracts of hill. In the tenth and eleventh centuries, a good deal of what is now Cumbria was under the control of Scotland. When *Domesday Book* was compiled in 1086, virtually all the area was outside the remit of the Norman scribes. The Norman Conquest was then extended to the north-west. The south-eastern area became the Barony of

Kendal, given to Yvo Talboise by a grateful conqueror. Yvo's neighbour in Furness was Roger, Count of Poitou. The Cartmel peninsula was retained by the Crown until 1186, being then granted to William, Earl of Pembroke. Subsequently, the Crown again took over the baronies of Carlisle, Kendal and Appleby. They became important elements in the new counties of Cumberland and Westmorland, with Furness, north of the sands of Morecambe Bay, associated with Lancashire.

Prior to the Conquest, Kirkby Kendale, 'the settlement with the church in the Kent valley,' was a thriving community, its church being one of the few covering a vast area. At Kendal, the Norman motte, on a hill about half a mile (0.8km) from the church, evolved as a castle. The influential family of Stricklands administered their estate from nearby Sizergh. Kendal received its market charter in 1189 and achieved the status of a borough early in the thirteenth century. Much of the local wealth was derived from wool. With the growth of monasteries, founded on the goodwill and copious gifts of money and land by the Norman lords, the wool trade became so important that Italian merchants, who had special trade concessions, purchased substantial quantities of the wool-clip. They valued the short staple of English wool.

In return for the many gifts, the monks undertook to pray for the souls of the donors in perpetuity. Furness Abbey, founded in the Vale of the Deadly Nightshade in 1127, was to become the second wealthiest Cistercian house after Fountains Abbey in Yorkshire, which also owned land in the Lake District. Furness had a grange, or outlying farm, in Borrowdale, hence the name Grange-in-Borrowdale for the village in the mouth of that famous dale. Furness kept innumerable sheep, which became known as herdwicks after their dalehead grazings. The monastery throve also on the

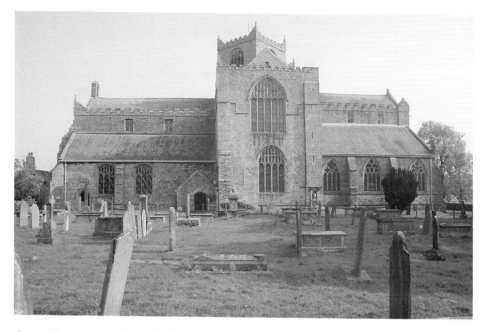

Cartmel Priory was founded by the Augustinian order at the end of the twelfth century. After the Dissolution of the Monasteries in 1537, the Priory Church of St Mary the Virgin was rescued and put to use as the Anglican parish church.

proceeds of manufacturing iron from locally mined ore.

Cartmel Priory (*walk 12*), an Augustinian house, was founded (1188) by William Marshall, Lord of Cartmel. To the priory, in early times, were brought, from the coastal settlements of Grange and Flookburgh, the bodies of those found drowned on Morecambe Bay. The monastic period was not one of enduring peace. Raids by the Scots in the twelfth century were attended by unimaginable savagery. A particularly gruesome episode was the massacre of people who had taken sanctuary in Kendal Church.

In the thirteenth century, Robert the Bruce and a force of Scotsmen swept down the coast and caused havoc at Cartmel before crossing the Sands to Lancaster, where town and castle were sacked. For a time,

the native red deer had to compete with sheep on the upland grazings. Then the sheep got the upper hand. The remaining red deer were either slaughtered or emparked. In 1225, a small park was created in the upper valley of the Trout Beck. The name was to be perpetuated in that of a farm, Troutbeck Park.

In the late fifteenth and early sixteenth centuries, following the Dissolution of the Monasteries, life became more settled, trade was liberalised and, with an increase in population, more land had to be 'taken in' from the waste. John Leland, who in the 1530s undertook fact-finding journeys and studied monastic records, referred to Kendal as 'a good market town'. He followed the course of the River Kent into the upper valley and crossed the Nan Bield Pass to reach Penrith.

In settled times, the landed gentry could show off their wealth and status by rebuilding in stone. A branch of the Phillipsons built the splendid Calgarth Hall and another constructed Rayrigg Hall (later to be owned by the Flemings). Phillipsons were esconsed at Hodge Hall, near Cartmel, where neighbouring families of means were the Thorpinstays of Thorphinsty Hall and Knypes of Burblethwaite Hall, two of the many old families about which little is heard today. At Graythwaite, west of Windermere, the Sandys were supreme.

Kendal's motto — *pannus mihi panis*, or 'wool is my bread' — reflected its importance as a textile centre. Much of the cloth was sold as 'cottons' to clothe the ordinary worker. A product of higher quality, which was dyed using a mixture of blue woad and yellow from a plant known as dyer's greenweed, became the celebrated Kendal Green. Shakespeare's Falstaff was visited by 'three misbegotten knaves in Kendal Green'.

South Lakeland retained much of its well-wooded state. In the late fifteenth century, the manor of Windermere had by-laws whereby dead timber might be taken for fuel, and trees specified by the lord's bailiff removed for repairing property or equipment. These 'woods of warrant' generally consisted of oak, ash and holly (a common woodland mix today). Alder and birch might be taken as fuel. Alder, incinerated in potash pits, produced an acceptable substitute for soap.

Kentmere Hall (walks 4, 5 &6) is a four-storey pele tower, with a vaulted cellar. Pele towers were commonly built in the fourteenth century to offer some protection against Scottish border raids, the farm animals being herded into the ground floor, and the farmer and his family taking refuge in the floors above. The dwelling alongside was built in the more settled times of the sixteenth century, replacing an earlier building.

In the seventeenth and eighteenth centuries, the woods were carefully managed to provide the iron industry with charcoal for smelting at sites known as 'bloomeries'. Tracts of woodland were clear-felled at regular intervals and, for charcoal-burning, sections of young trees were carefully stacked in 'pits' and covered with sods. These pits were ignited when a central pole was removed and a fire kindled in the void. The woods yielded timber for the production of swills (agricultural baskets) and oak bark for the tanning industry. Fisheries were important. The annual run of salmon and sea trout was intercepted and, by the Leven, overflow of Windermere, eels were trapped on moonless autumn nights. Morecambe Bay's stocks of fish (also shrimps, cockles and mussels) were exploited by fisherfolk who evolved a technique of operating at low tide using horses and carts.

The Civil War had little effect on the area. Much more significant in the seventeenth century was the upward sweep of adherence to Nonconformity. The evangelical zeal of the Dissenters brought a breath of fresh air to the stuffy Established Church. George Fox, founder of the Quakers, knew South Lakeland and Furness well. It was from this area that many of Quakerism's original supporters came. In 1658, after gathering in each other's homes, the Quakers opened a meeting house at Colthouse, near Hawkshead. Soon, Parliament was curbing religious freedom by restricting the size of services, by insisting that the Book of Common Prayer should be used, and by not hesitating to fine or imprison those who offended against the law. Among them was Fox himself. The Five Mile Act, forbidding Nonconformist gatherings within five miles of a parish church, led to the appearance of Quaker and Baptist meeting places in remote spots.

In politically settled times following the Civil War, the Lake District experienced a building boom which brought into being a host of attractive, stone- and slate-built yeoman's houses and farms. Today, they give the Lakeland valleys and fellsides much of their character. The yeoman farmers (who were later so much admired by William Wordsworth, Lakeland's poet) were virtually self-sufficient and gloried in their independence. In the eighteenth century, when Kendal was without doubt the most important town in Westmorland, raw materials and goods were shifted on the backs of up to 350 packhorses. Teams of packhouses traded with London, and every six weeks there was a service between Kendal and Glasgow. A team of six packhorses made the journey from Kendal to Hawkshead twice a week, linking with a service from Hawkshead to Whitehaven.

A crucial link in the packhorse system was the ancient ferry, powered by men using long oars, which crossed Windermere from a point just south of Bowness, in Westmorland, to a nab on the Lancashire side. In 1635, when the ferryboat sank, forty-seven people were drowned. The herringbone pattern of wavelets was left by larger boats transporting iron ore in bulk to the 'bloomeries'. Backbarrow, in the valley of the Leven, was the setting in 1711 of the first blast furnace to be built in the North. (The Backbarrow Ironworks were in production until 1965.)

In the nineteenth century, a brisk demand for bobbins by the textile industry in Lancashire created a further demand for young trees to be carefully managed. A classic survival of a bobbin mill is Stott Park, near Lakeside. Much of Lakeland was denuded by the demands of industry. Elsewhere, the natural regeneration of timber was prevented by the incessant nibbling of sheep. Towards the end of the eighteenth century, Nathaniel Spencer, travelling beside Windermere, noticed that 'the south east shores are covered with wood, cut into distinct

Packhorse bridges were built from before the Norman Conquest to around the end of the eighteenth century, to enable the packhorse trains of up to forty animals, travelling around 15 miles (25km) per day, to traverse difficult river crossings. The bridges, such as this graceful example which links an ancient packhorse route over the River Kent to the Nan Bield Pass, were usually narrow and built without parapets, so that the panniers slung either side of the horses were not dislodged.

plantations, and running to the top of lofty mountains.'

It was the beginning of a trend which was to transform the environs of Windermere. The Browne family of Town End, Troutbeck, planted quick-growing conifers on their estate as early as 1783. They chose Scots pine, with some exotic firs, including the white American spruce. The Curwens of Belle Island afforested Claife Heights with 30,000 larches in 1798. Bishop Watson smothered Gummers How with larch (1805 and subsequent years). Pines and larches, in large numbers, were introduced to the Brathay estate at the head of the lake. The sycamore and beech trees which are now so much a part of Lakeland scenery are from stock introduced in the eighteenth century.

In the second half of the eighteenth century, Kendal's many inns were lively, catering for the the coaching service which connected the town with Liverpool, Leeds, Penrith, Whitehaven, Warrington and London. A Kendal–London coach completed the journey in three days, the cost per head being £3. Towards the end of the eighteenth century, and through into the nineteenth, Lakeland was 'discovered' by those with leisure and means to travel who, being prevented by war with the French from undertaking the Grand Tour, discovered from writings and illustrations that picturesque landscape existed in Britain.

13

Visiting the Lakes also offered an escape from the Industrial Revolution, which had blighted many parts of the land. The first tourists took advantage of the turnpike road from Kendal through the heart of the district, where rockscapes and swirling mists allowed the sensitive to experience a gamut of emotions.

This was also a period of agricultural improvement, as evidenced by the enclosure of the commons with drystone walls. The small yeoman farmers who had managed the Lakeland landscape for many years were now in decline. Wordsworth recorded a halving of the number of 'statesmen' between the years 1770 and 1820. In such civilised areas as Windermere's eastern shore,

Whilst mechanisation has in recent years eased the Lakeland farmer's burden, there are still specialised tasks requiring skills unchanged over the centuries, such as the construction or repair of drystone walls, as here in the Winster Valley.

the Georgian period was a time when mini-mansions with well-manicured grounds were constructed for the wealthy, including the new-rich of the Industrial Revolution.

Lakeland already had buildings with a classical form. Thomas English, a merchant from Nottingham, built a circular residence on Belle Island (1774) and Richard Watson moved into a new mansion at Calgarth Park (1789). Storrs Hall (1790) stood to the south of Bowness, its land extending to the lakeshore where, on a stone causeway, appeared an octagonal garden house, honouring admirals of the Napoleonic Wars. The structure, clearly visible from lake traffic, was called Storrs Temple. It was a fiercely patriotic age. A battlemented tower commemorating the admirals was built on Finsthwaite Knott, overlooking Lakeside.

Kendal developed into the 'auld grey town', built largely of limestone. A visitor from the south passed through Kirkland to Highgate (the 'gate' being a street) and on to Stricklandgate (named after the Stricklands of Sizergh). With a railway junction at Oxenholme, Kendal was handy to the line extending to Birthwaite (re-named Windermere, and soon in lusty growth towards townhood). The rail expansion of 1847 stimulated the growth of other little communities such as Bowness and Ambleside.

The presiding genius of Lakeland was William Wordsworth. A neighbour, Harriet Martineau, who settled at the Knoll, Ambleside, became another star in Lakeland's literary firmament. She was visited by many literary celebrities, including George Eliot and Charlotte Brontë. Harriet's *Guide to Windermere* came out as human settlement in the area was under speedy evolution, following the arrival of the railway. She detected a need for a revised guide and considered she was the best person to write it!

During the Edwardian twilight, a special Windermere class of yacht was devised for

Kendal has been a thriving community for over a thousand years, now providing for the needs of tourists rather than the woollen industry, while still retaining its market-town character.

the lake and racing was a rich man's sport. The well-to-do extended the elegance of their homes to the lake when they had fine steamboats built for them. A novel feature, made of copper, was the Windermere Kettle, heated by water from the steam engine and guaranteed to come to boiling point in three minutes. In 1912, Bowness was the second town in Britain (after Preston) to instal electric street lighting, the power coming from a waterwheel at Trout-beck Bridge.

Windermere had a role to play during Second World War, when the steamer *Tern* became a naval vessel, renamed HMS *Undine*, and patrolled during the years when Sunderland Flying Boats, assembled at White Cross Bay by the Short Brothers, were flown off the lake.

In 1951, the Lake District was designated as a National Park, the board being charged with the preservation of the land-scape and providing facilities for its enjoyment by the public. Kendal was the administrative centre of Westmorland, and thriving with the presence of K Shoes and Provincial Insurance. In 1974, the name Westmorland was lost under boundary changes which brought in the county of Cumbria.

The past twenty years have seen massive social changes, with a rapid increase in tourism, a notable expansion of attractions for visitors, an ageing population and an incursion in many villages of retired couples with new bungalows. Kendal has maintained its prosperity. Windermere might have 1,000 craft of various kinds on it at peak season, yet provides quiet bays for immigrant waterfowl in winter. Much of the landscape remains unsullied and is a delight for walkers.

WILDLIFE

Natural history is diverse in an area extending from fell country which clears 2,000 feet (600m), as at the head of Kentmere and Longsleddale, to the mudflats of Morecambe Bay, a vast tidal inlet. On the high hills, birdlife is sparse and few species of plant are able to cope with the acid conditions. Conversely, the bay may look desolate, but in fact it teems with diminutive forms of life which sustains in winter a huge congregation of wading birds and waterfowl, with knot and dunlin providing spectacular flying displays for walkers on the promenade at Grange-over-Sands (*walk 12*).

The fell country has grandeur, and is the nesting place of several species of bird which command respect. In winter, the ravens are ever-active, riding the updraught and sometimes, with great verve, flicking on their backs, then returning to a normal flying position. The peregrine is now relatively common. Of the mammals, the largest of the native terrestrial creature is the red deer, which long ago adapted itself to the bleak fells around the head of Mardale. Footloose stags wander into Mosedale and the head of Kentmere (*walks 5 and 6*).

Do not take for granted the horned sheep of the hill country, for they are here by the right of hundreds of generations. The breeds to look for in the Lake District are herdwick (small, white-faced, coarse-fleeced, stocky legs), Rough Fell (mottled face, confined to the dry, slatey fells of the south-east) and the Swaledale (black face, grey around the muzzle, compact fleece, a type of crag sheep 'fixed' by Pennine farmers).

The deciduous woods of south-east Lakeland, once clear-felled every fifteen years or so to make charcoal or to sustain industries like bobbin-making, are neglected. They give sanctuary to the badger, roe deer and squirrel. The badger, familiar to everyone through photographs and films, is rarely seen during the day, emerging from its sett at what the old folk picturesquely called 'the edge o' dark'. The red squirrel, a dainty creature with long tufty ears, was until recently locally common all the way down to the woodland beside Morecambe Bay. The grey squirrel, larger, less specialist in food requirements and with short rounded ears, has moved in to the Lake District and is now as far north as Grasmere.

The clean, fast-flowing rivers, such as Sprint and Kent (*walk 4*), have good stocks of the white-clawed crayfish, so called to distinguish this native from the introduced American variety. The rivers also provide a living for the dipper, a bird which is small, dumpy, dark, with a white 'bib', and a fidgety nature which gives the impression it is doing press-ups while perched on water-washed boulders. The otter is doing quite well in the South-East Lakes now that the hunting pressure has been lifted, rivers cleaned up and artificial holts (riverside holes used for sanctuary and to raise young) constructed. Otters are regularly seen in the Kent below Kendal (*walk 1*).

The southern limestone area, where pearl-white scars and pavements give the hills their shape and appearance, has a varied butterfly population. In the woods are red, roe and fallow deer. Morecambe Bay's rich birdlife may be appreciated handily from such places as the promenades at Arnside (*walk 10*) or Grange (*walk 12*). At the last-named, the lake in the ornamental gardens holds a range of waterfowl, with named pictures for identification. The species include the elegant pintail, the drake being grey, with a chocolate-brown head and white underparts extending as a white stripe up the sides of the neck. Kendal's natural history museum is another

Lakeland is one of the last strongholds of the red squirrel. If the walker is privileged to see one, it is most likely to be in mixed deciduous woodland, such as Craggy Wood, Staveley.

17

prime source of information; here, too, are stimulating displays.

In the Silverdale area (*walk 10*) is a range of woodland birds. A mile or two south of the Cumbrian border lies Leighton Moss, a reserve of the Royal Society for the Protection of Birds, which includes among its fauna the bittern, a heron-like bird with a colouring (to quote a young visitor) like burnt toast and a voice which is deep and resonant, like a foghorn. Also on the reserve is another scarce bird, the bearded tit, a denizen of the whispering reedbeds. In summer, at Leighton Moss, deer and otter watches are organised at dusk.

The Cumbria Wildlife Trust is now based at Brockhole, the National Park Visitor Centre.

Some Typical Bird Habitats

Open fells (*walks 6 and 7*)   The meadow pipit, commonest bird of the high fells, is small and streaky brown, most easily

Ravens nest in high, craggy areas, where they make their nests from twigs, lined with sheep wool. Its call — a husky pruk pruk *— draws attention to this glossy-black bird.*

recognised from its behaviour at nesting time. It has a conspicuous song flight, singing both during the ascent and descent. On the way back to earth, the bird holds its wings and tail stiffly out and resembles a shuttlecock. The nest is tucked away in rank grass. A walker who unwittingly goes near a nest is surprised when the sitting bird rises at the very last moment. Small flocks of wintering snow buntings (of Icelandic origin) flicker across the austere uplands like snowflakes, for they are predominantly white. They dine on grass seeds, especially *mollinia*.

The raven is identifiable by its large size, coal-black plumage and bill as tough as a pickaxe. The glossy plumage picks up silvery highlights. Ravens are denizens of high craggy areas. If you are close to a bird (and sometimes one will sweep by you at close range), you might see the shaggy throat and the wedge-shaped tail. The throaty voice of the raven — *prruk, prruk* — draws attention to it as it rides a cushion of air sweeping up from the dale. Family parties of birds are especially playful with each other. Sometimes, a raven closes its wings and, giving a husky call, drops in the air for a short distance before opening them again. The twiggy nest is usually on a ledge where there is a precipitous cliff. The nesting season begins early, and the young hatch out in late March or early April, a time of plenty on the fellsides from the corpses of sheep which succumbed to the winter.

On rocky hillsides and where there are walls, the wheatear may be seen. The conspicuous cock bird is bluey-grey above. There is a flitting flight and a harsh *chack chack* call. The dipper, most often seen on rivers and becks in the dales, occurs at quite high elevations, such as the beck which deals with the outflow of Skeggles Water, between Kentmere and Longsleddale (*walk 4*).

Limestone hills   The 250 acre (100ha) Whitbarrow reserve of the Cumbria Wild-

life Trust occupies the highest part of the summit plateau of the hill of that name which sprawls to the north of the A590 west of Levens Bridge (*walk 13*). Botanists are inclined to visit Whitbarrow in spring. For the birdwatcher, quiet winter days often repay a visit. It is then that large flocks of fieldfare and redwing gather. These Scandinavian thrushes, which winter in Britain, have a nomadic life dictated by the availability of food. The fieldfare resembles a mistle thrush in some respects but has a blue-grey head and rump, and blackish tail. There is a 'chacking' flight call. The redwing, which is much smaller, is best identified with regard to its white eye-stripe. The name comes from the reddish-brown of flanks and wing, which are most visible when the bird is in flight. The flight-note of the redwing is a thin piping call.

A nature reserve called Brown Robin, at the southern end of a limestone escarpment beyond the Netherwood Hotel, Grange-over-Sands, is the nesting place of treecreeper, nuthatch and green woodpecker. The treecreeper, brown above, silverish below, squats at the base of a tree trunk, then makes an erratic ascent, stopping here and there to probe in cracks and crannies with a beak which is delicate and slightly decurved. From a distance, the bird resembles a mouse in its movements. A nuthatch, blue-grey above, buff below, fares well from the food put out on bird tables by householders. The bird can walk up and down the trunk of a tree with equal facility.

Deciduous woodland (*walks 12 and 18*)
The buzzard is fairly common. Quite large, brownish with broad wings which are inclined to curl upwards at the ends, it rides the air currents and, when calling, utters a cat-like mewing. The pied flycatcher is a summer visitor, the male sporting black on the head and upper parts, and white forming a patch on each wing and the sides

The red deer is the largest of our native mammals, but despite its considerable size — up to fifty inches (120cm) at the shoulder — and the stag's antler spread, the animal is often overlooked in woodland and on the fellside, where it relies on immobility to escape detection. There is an appreciable difference in size between a big Furness stag and a leaner one which subsists in wild fell country such as Martindale.

of the tail. The female is drab by comparison. Notice also how, like other flycatchers, the bird is fond of flirting its tail and darts from a perch to intercept passing insects for food.

The old woods, where today little management takes place and fallen trees often lie and rot, attract woodcock, which nests on a carpet of last year's oak leaves and is most difficult to locate because of its cryptic coloration and ability to stay quite still for long periods. One poacher claimed to identify a sitting bird by the sparkle in its eye. In woodcock country, such as Dorothy Farrer's Spring Wood, on a south-facing slope near Staveley (*walk 3*), you may see the cock bird fly around its territory at dusk, periodically calling (it sounds like three grunts and a squeak). This custom is known as 'roding'.

Deciduous woods provide abundant food (insects and grubs) for titmice and woodpeckers. All the common tits — great, blue, coal and marsh — are seen here. The great tit is black on its head and has a broad black stripe on its yellow underparts. A blue tit is familiar to anyone with a bird-table at home. This lively bird has bright blue on its head. The coal tit looks less smart and has black on its head but white at the cheeks and nape. The marsh tit is also less bright than the first two, having a black crown and chin and brownish body, paler on the underparts.

Arnside (*walk 10*) is a prime birdwatching area, the interest extending from the profusion of shore birds to those of woodland, such as Beachwood, an easy walk from the village (Beachwood Lane, off Red Hills Road). Look for the redpoll and bullfinch. These woods have long-tailed tits the year through. The species nests here and wintering flocks may be seen. Grubbins Wood, west of Arnside, by the Kent Estuary, is a breeding place of blackcap and goldcrest, bullfinch, green woodpecker, tawny owl and jay. Nesting boxes provided by the Cumbria Wildlife Trust attract great and blue tits. This wood, like many another with a good stock of yew trees, which produce vermilion berries, is attractive to redwings, fieldfares and (at times) waxwings, also known as the Bohemian chatterer, a brownish, starling-sized bird with a prominent crest and grey rump. A flock of feeding waxwings is usually indifferent to humans who watch them from a range of a few yards.

A woodland nature reserve some two miles (3km) south of Kendal on the A65 is named after Enid Maples and consists of a plantation made as recently as 1979. There is a rich variety of tree species and good numbers of common woodland birds. Among them are willow warbler, spotted flycatcher and garden warbler.

Coniferous woodland   Stroll in an area where there are larch plantations (*walk 17*) in the 'off' season and you might hear the thin calling — *zee-zee-zee* — of a goldcrest, more precisely a 'charm' of goldcrests, busily calling as they look for food high in the trees. This is our smallest bird. The bird has a dumpy form and, on its crown, a yellow stripe bordered by black stripes. In the company of goldcrests there may be an assortment of titmice — blue, coal — with a treecreeper bringing up the rear. The blue tit is familiar to all as a regular visitor to both urban and countryside gardens in winter. The coal, which is slightly smaller (though you are unlikely to notice this in the wild), is distinguished by its black crown and white nape.

Mossland   Meathop and Catcrag Mosses, which lie between the A590 and Kent Estuary (*seen from walk 13*), are raised peat bogs which were among those affected by the construction of the Furness Railway, and also land reclamation and drainage. The consequences have been a drying out of the mosses and their invasion by trees, mainly pine and birch. The Cumbria Wildlife Trust has on lease 150 acres (60ha). Birds of the open areas include the curlew, instantly recognisable by its large size and long, curved bill, the shelduck (green head, chestnut on mantle, shoulders and breast, otherwise white) and the heron, a bird familiar to most people and notable for its large size, long neck and legs, and greyish plumage. Birds of the wooded parts of Meathop Moss include the buzzard, sparrowhawk and jay, with the willow warbler, a visitor for breeding, much in evidence as a songster in spring.

Rivers and lakes The Kent (*walk 1*) and lesser rivers — the Crayke and the Eea in the Cartmel Valley (*walk 12*) — have their compliment of dippers. Dipper haunts are also favoured by the grey wagtail, a slim, long-tailed, active little bird is blue-grey above, yellow beneath and with white outer tail-feathers. The male has a black gorget. Some riverside birds, such as waterhen and mallard, have suffered at nesting time from the attention of feral mink. The heron nests in some of the southern valleys and at Dallam, near Milnthorpe.

Bowness Bay (*walk 19*) is the area of maximum concentration of waterbirds, the attraction being — food. Here, swans frequently lumber ashore and mingle with the daytrippers. At times, the large birds are obscured by the bodies of people leaving the steamer pier. It is not wise to go too close to a swan, which can have a savage peck and if irritated can inflict damage with a blow from its wings. The fact that the Bowness swans are so confiding should not be taken to mean that they are never peevish. Generally they restrict themselves to tugging at your clothes if you have some food left in your hand. Much less confiding are the whooper swans which visit the lakes in winter, though less frequently than they

did. In recent years, there have been massive concentrations of whooper swans (and their far northern cousins, the Bewicks swan) at reserves, notably Caerlaveroch (to the north) and Martin Mere (to the south). Once, the sight of a family party of Icelandic whooper swans quietly feeding on lake edge vegetation was a regular attraction in the Lake District.

Canada geese, introduced from the New World several centuries ago to beautify the grounds of big houses, are locally numerous. Greylags, reintroduced as a nesting species through the efforts of wildfowlers at a reserve at the Duddon Estuary, nest in various places and are seen out-of-season from Humphrey Head (*walk 11*). Some geese use the central Lakeland flyway when migrating. This takes them over Windermere.

Other Wildlife

Mammals The red deer is reported from Meathop and other mossland by the Kent Estuary, also from Whitbarrow (*walk 13*) and woods in the Finsthwaite area, near Newby Bridge, where Windermere outflows. The red deer has a 'plastic' quality, adjusting its size to suit the terrain and feeding conditions. So the animals frequenting lowland woods in South-East Lakeland are appreciably larger than those of the open fell further north.

Roe deer, the smallest (so far!) of the free-range deer in the Lake District, are ubiquitous. A hoarse bark heard in deciduous woodland might be the alarm call of a roe buck. Look for the roe in the twilight. In late winter into spring, which is a lean time for mammals, roe may be seen grazing in fields adjacent to woodland, quite close to a large place like Ambleside. The highlying Hervey Reserve, on Whitbarrow (*walk 13*), is a roe haunt, but the woods near Grange-over-Sands (*walk 12*) hold quite large numbers. Fallow deer occur in the woods of the Silverdale area (*walk 10*) and are emparked at Holker, Dallam and Levens parks. (The Holker and Dallam animals are of the light phase. Those in Levens (*walk 1*) are melanistic and usually referred to as being black.)

Our Lakeland red squirrel, under threat from the more robust grey squirrel, which was introduced from America, is being given special encouragement by the Cumbrian Wildlife Trust and other interested organisations. Red squirrels occur where there are suitable deciduous woods, especially those with an abundance of hazel. The species is now scarce in Southern Lakeland, where the grey squirrel has gained the upper hand. Reserves of the Cumbrian Wildlife Trust with stocks of red squirrels are Dorothy Farrer's Spring Wood, a mile (1.6km) east of Staveley, and also Whitbarrow (*walk 13*). The greys seem to breed faster and are less finicky about what they eat, finding alternative supplies in a bad winter. The red, a more specialist feeder, suffered from the consequences of the Dutch elm disease, elm keys being an important food supply in June. The Wildlife Trust makes use of special food hoppers which are accessible to the red but reject the heavier greys.

The red fox, which is a prominent part of Lake District folklore through the huntsman John Peel and his disciples, is much commoner than many suppose but, with its finely-tuned senses of smell and hearing, usually contrives to keep out of sight of human visitors. In recent years, the resident foxes have been augmented by animals caught up in urban areas by well-meaning but thoughtless people and released in the wild. Brock, the badger, our little English bear, lumbers through the woods at twilight. Early morning joggers sometimes encounter the badger, which is generally nocturnal. Rabbits are a useful food source for fox, stoat and weasel, and also

*Flatfish caught using a rod and line at Arnside (*walk 10*) are known locally as a fluke.*

for birds of prey, notably the buzzard. The rabbit population varies according to the incidence of disease, but at the time of writing the population is high. Feral mink are a problem in some areas but easily caught using baited cage-traps.

Amphibians Fellwalkers are often surprised to find frogs around pools and tarns on the tops. Both frogs and palmate newts occur in the tarn on Whitbarrow (*walk 13*). Toads have been found at a tarn on Barkbooth Lot, in the Winster Valley (*walk 14*). The palmate newt is one of three species found in the ponds of Grange-over-Sands

23

park (*walk 12*), the other species being the smooth and crested.

Lizards and grass snakes occur at Ash Landing, a nature reserve half a mile (o.8km) south of Ferry House, on the west bank of Windermere. Slow worms have been seen in the gardens of Grange. The common lizard occurs in the Cartmel Valley. The adder, a snake which is recognisable because of a zigzag dark mark along its back, occurs on drier grasslands and heaths. The adder is a sensitive and rather shy snake which does not usually attack unless provoked. Its bite causes much pain in a human victim, though rarely ends in death.

Butterflies and moths The main butterfly haunts are to the south of the area covered — on the limestone hills and the mosses bordering Kent Estuary and Morecambe Bay. Arnside Knott (*walk 10*) is notable for the Scotch argus, as well as the brown argus, grayling and duke of burgundy. The Scotch argus, which flies in August and September, is a dark brown butterfly, with an orange-red band adorned by white-centred black spots. The dark colour allows it to absorb more heat from the sun than a lighter hue. The grayling is a paler brown, with yellow-orange band and black spots. The high brown fritillary, which is very local in the North Country, might be seen, among other places, at Whitbarrow (*walk 13*).

Flowers in local meadows attract peacock, red admiral, brimstone, orange tip, wall, meadow brown, small tortoiseshell, painted lady and whites. In the grounds of Sizergh Castle (National Trust), near Kendal is a tract of ground, formerly lawn, which has been allowed to develop local species of flowering plants and grasses. It has proved attractive to butterflies of many species. On Meathop Moss are large heath, emperor, oak eggar, green hairstreak, wood tiger, footman and clouded buff. The caterpillar of the emperor moth, which feeds on heather, has a splendid colour scheme, being bright green with black marks between rows of black-bristled, yellow warts round the body. These are interspersed with orange rings. The moth has a showy coloration, featuring two big 'eyes' on a white background and two smaller eyes.

Latterbarrow, beside the old stretch of road adjacent to the Derby Arms Hotel at Witherslack, (*walk 13*) is notable for its high brown and pearl-bordered fritillaries, and also grassland species — grayling and northern brown argus, a small dark butterfly, the caterpillars of which include rock rose on their menu. The Hervey Reserve on Whitbarrow (*walk 13*) holds a variety of butterflies in summer, including both high brown and dark green fritillaries, brimstone, northern brown argus and small blue. Gummers How (*walk 15*) is especially well-known among naturalists for its green hairstreaks.

Insects Grubbins Wood, just west of Arnside (*walk 10*), is one of several old tracts of woodland holding the large mounds made by the wood ant. The glow-worm, now scarce in the North Country, has been reported from Barkbooth Lot nature reserve (*walk 14*), a mile (1.6km) north of Bowland Bridge. A small tarn at Barkbooth Lot holds several species of damsel fly.

limestone to the south. Wild flowers should be left *in situ*, to give pleasure to many.

Some Typical Plant Habitats

Nowhere in South-East Lakeland does the elevation of the fells overtop the 2,700 feet (823m) contour. There is no permanent snow cover. The climate at high elevation is harsh, but Lakeland is usually wrapped in the moist air from the sea which is found on three sides of the country. Silurian soils being poor in nutrients and relatively acid, much of the ground which is clear of rock is covered by coarse grasses and bracken. These areas are not particularly rich florally. There is little to interest the visitor who would like to see as many flowering plants as possible in a holiday period. The best areas for plants are undoubtedly on the

High fells The loss of tree cover and leaching debased the fells in distant times. In modern days, over-grazing by sheep has, in some cases, reduced heather moorland to a waste of coarse grasses like *Nardus stricta*, which is unpalatable to sheep. Well represented in the relatively poor flora of the high fells is alpine ladies mantle, which is a creeping plant with yellow-green flowers, the leaves green above, silvery and hairy below. Along the southern edge of the Volcanics, at the head of Longsleddale (*walk 7*) and Kentmere (*walks 5 and 6*), are boulder fields sporting ferns, including the well-named parsley fern, though this plant is much more common in the Ambleside

The commonest species of heather, ling or Calluna vulgaris, *provides a splash of summer colour to many Lakeland areas. It is distinguished from the other heather species — cross-leaved heath — by its low, shrubby apperance, smaller and paler purple flowers, and minute leaves.*

area. Species of polypody are found on rock faces in the shaded gills. On the stream banks, in both valleys, grows the lemon-scented mountain fern.

On Gummers How (*walk 15*) and the knolls of Potter Fell (*walk 3*) are remnant patches of ling, with blaeberry. Upland mosses are less extensive than they were. Wet, acidy grassland is a good place for rushes. Bogbean, with a stout creeping underwater rhizome, or root-like stem, short flowering stems and pink or white flowers, occurs in the wet flushes and is petalled in late June and early July.

Limestone country   June is a good time to visit the limestone, notably at Scout Scar, near Kendal (*walk 2*), and Whitbarrow, near Witherslack (*walk 13*). Move with special care, especially when the limestone is wet, and do not attempt to explore the scars themselves, which should be left to the rock-climbing fraternity. Species of plant like the dropwort and rock rose occur in limestone terrain. Dropwort, an erect plant with relatively few leaves, is topped by six white petals, which has a flowering season from May to August. Rock rose, with its yellow flowers which emerge in June, is the food plant of the brown argus butterfly. Growing on cliffs at Scout Scar and on Whitbarrow, and flowering in May, is the rare hoary rock rose. Scout Scar is composed of limestone but heather occurs in little pockets, a consequence of heavy rainfall and the leaching of the soils.

The Cumbrian Wildlife Trust's reserve on Whitbarrow, named after Canon G A K Hervey, who founded the organisation in 1962, is in the main covered by blue moor grass and boasts species such as limestone bedstraw, salad burnet and wild thyme. Limestone pavement, a relatively scarce geological feature, found at the aforementioned sites — also on Hampsfell and Cartmel Fell (*walk 12*) — hold within their

grykes (the crevices between blocks, which are known as clints) the remnants of an old woodland flora and much else. Blue sesleria grass dominates much of the Hervey Reserve on Whitbarrow. The dark red helleborine, with its deep purple flowers, is an especially showy plant. The Scotch argus (local and somewhat rare in England) is attracted to a species of grass, *Sesleria albicans*. On limestone pavement, where there is a scattering of hazel, wood sage, a dwarf hairy shrub with greenish-yellow flowers, is found. Elsewhere, look for the familiar birds-foot trefoil and thyme. On

Limestone pavements contain a varied plantlife, which is sheltered from the extremes of the weather.

the sparsely vegetated areas of outcropping limestone grow wood sorrel, its white flowers having pale lilac veins, and herb robert, with bright pink flowers. Other plants to be seen in the spring are wood anemone, lesser meadow rue, maindenhair, green spleenwort and rigid buckler fern. On the ledges of limestone cliffs grow spring sandwort, sporting white flowers, and small meadow-rue, its clustering, tiny white flowers having yellow stamens.

Limestone grassland At Scout Scar (*walk 2*), fragrant orchids are locally numerous. Latterbarrow, just off the cul-de-sac formed by the old A590 near the Derby Arms, is a reserve consisting of ten acres (4ha) of limestone grassland, supporting over 160 species of flowering plant, including rock rose, with its comparatively large yellow flowers, salad burnet, with its greenish flowers and greyish leaves, kidney vetch, fellwort and (abundantly) cowslips. A visit to Sizergh Castle, south-west of Kendal, in the spring is illuminating because a tract of limestone grassland is left unmown until late in the season, allowing local varieties to set their seed. Orchids are numerous.

Woodland At bluebell time, many of the woods of South-East Lakeland are wondrously transformed. Where there is a base-rich soil, plant life is varied and profuse. Many woods were originally coppiced, being clear-felled every fifteen years or so, the wood to be used for the production of charcoal or to sustain local crafts. Where the cover is still thin, and the ground is well-lit, the flowering plants include dogs mercury, ramsons (often referred to as 'garlic'), lords-and-ladies and early purple orchid.

The wild daffodils of Brigsteer Woods, flanking Scout Scar (*walk 2*), were made famous by Mrs Humphry Ward, a Victorian novelist, in *Helbeck of Bannisdale*, where she wrote of a Westmorland wood in daffodil time, with:

> the golden flowers, the slim stalks [rising] from a mist of greenish-blue, made by their speary leaf amid the encircling browns and purples, the intricate stem and branch-work of the still winter-bound hazels ... They were flung on the fell-side ... in sheets and tapestries of gold — such an audacious, unreckoned plenty as went strangely with the frugal air and temper of the northern country, with the bare walled fields, the ruggedness of the crags above and the melancholy of the treeless marsh below.

At Grubbins Wood, a reserve of the Cumbria Wildlife Trust,

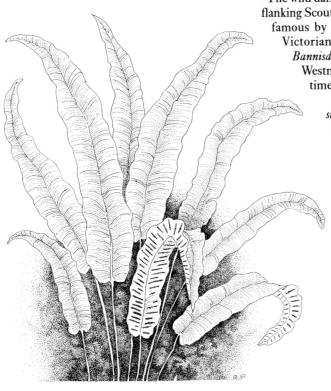

Harts tongue fern is easily recognised by its broad, fleshy, shiny fronds. This woodland plant also occurs in areas of exposed limestone, growing in the deep grykes and so avoiding being grazed by sheep.

Deciduous woodland areas such as Rigmaden Park (walk 9) are a magical experience in springtime, their quiet, shady glades carpeted by bluebells. Capturing the 'blueness' of these familiar plants on camera is not as easy as you might think: the flowers come out as pink if taken in direct sunlight, so pick a shaded area.

ground which was originally coppiced has been neglected for over seventy years, and a limestone escarpment with a thin soil was laid down as glacial drift from Lakeland. This gives acid conditions in a limestone setting. In the area are herb paris, solitary and erect with prominent oval leaves, green and stinking helleborine, solomons seal, with lance-like leaves and white bell-shaped flowers, baneberry, columbine, lily-of-the-valley, early purple orchid, common spotted orchid and butterfly orchid. Of the many ferns, harts tongue is extremely common. The hard fern is associated with the acid soils.

Grassland Lime-rich meadowland which has not had modern fertilisers applied may yield an astonishing succession of wild flowers. In March and April, the species to look for are wood anemone, with its

big white flowers, violet, celandine, primrose and wild daffodil. May brings ramsons, early purple orchid, crosswort and bluebell. In June, the accent is on spotted orchid, twayblade, ox-eye daisy, bistort, columbine, and in late summer there is meadowsweet, knapweed, St Johns wort, betony and meadow vetchling, the last-named plant having conspicuous yellow flowers and lance-like leaves. At Merlewood, near Grange-over-Sands, grow rock rose, thyme, fairy flax and salad burnet. Cowslips and primroses occur along the woodland edges. Where the ground is steep and leaching has occurred, look for knapweed during the flowering season.

Riverside, tarn and mossland An excursion beside the Kent below Kendal towards Levens Bridge (*walk 1*) reveals a lusty colonisation of giant hogweed and Himalayan balsam. Plants of special interest include the yellow star of Bethlehem, the bell-shaped flowers of which are to be seen from March to May. Bluebells grow from the turf by Kentmere Tarn (*walk 4*). On mossland, sphagnum, a dominant species, is the great peat-forming plant, being associated with bog asphodel, with its spike-like cluster of yellow flowers and sword-shaped leaves in two ranks. Also present will be bog rosemary, a dwarf shrub with drooping flowers, bright pink fading to white. Cranberry, cotton sedge and two heathers — cross-leaved heath where it is moist, and ling on the drier areas — give what is an acid area its annual period of brightness. Look also for bog myrtle, sundew and purple moor-grass.

Tree Species

The glacial ice retreated from the Lake District some 10,000 years ago. As the landscape became green, an open scrub contained juniper and willow, which gave way to birch. Another early settler, hazel, was swamped by the development of oak forest which swaddled the valleys (except the wettest areas, where alder was dominant) and extended up the fellsides to an elevation of about 2,000 feet (610m). The largest threat to the ancient forest came from man who, from an early period, cleared trees. The Norse settlement of the ninth and tenth centuries created permanently open areas (thwaites) in the upper dales. The teeth of sheep prevented natural regeneration. Timber was felled to be made into charcoal for iron smelting. Deciduous woodland was coppiced for many years up to about eight decades ago. They were clear-felled every fifteen years or so and, neglected, have now grown into a tangled mass.

Coniferous   The first big plantings took place in the eighteenth century. Larch was popular. Geriatric larch are to be seen on

Giant hogweed is an umbellifer capable of growing to well over eight feet (2.5m). Walkers should leave the plant alone, for its sap can cause skin irritations.

the flanks of Gummers How (*walk 15*). The Forestry Commission, formed in 1919, achieved a strong commercial interest in the area. The main forests, planted to the west of Windermere and to the north, made use of species imported from north-west America — sitka spruce, lodge-pole pine. The formal appearance of the plantations distressed conservationists and led, in 1935, to agreement that henceforth no more planting would be taken in Central Lakeland. Grizedale, near Hawkshead, became a major forest. The commission has planted timber on Whitbarrow (*walk 2*). Meathop Moss, between Whitbarrow and the Kent Estuary, was planted with conifers. They have so soaked up moisture that the old mossland character of a sodden terrain has been changed to one in which self-sown trees might flourish.

Scots pine, the only member of its family which is a native of Britain, has a lanky form and bottle-green needles. Old trees have an orange appearance high on the trunk where the bark has peeled.

Deciduous   Typical trees of a Lakeland deciduous wood are sessile oak, birch and rowan. The silver birch is a common tree, not only in established forests but in areas of quarrying, where it roots readily on the waste heaps, as in upper Kentmere (*walk 5*). At Grubbins Wood, near Arnside (*walk 10*), the acid glacial soil overlying limestone holds durmast oak, beech, ash and small-leaved lime. A shrub layer includes holly, hazel, rowan and thorn. Flowering shrubs include guelder rose, cherry, spindle, white-beam — which is familiar as an adornment to urban streets — purling and alder-leaved buckthorn. The service tree, characterised by a dark brown bark fissured with pale grey scales, is here near its northern limit. A colony exists at Grubbins Wood. Some of the limestone cliffs, such as Whitbarrow (*walk 13*), are screened by native woodland, which is mainly birch with an under-storey of juniper.

Exotics   Trees planted by the great landowners are not without interest. In the gardens of Grange-over-Sands (*walk 12*) are such trees as ginkgo, davidia (the handkerchief trees, so named because of the visual effect of the white bracts), dawn redwood and Indian bean. At Merlewood and Hampsfield, near Grange, redwoods and sequoias have attained a height of about 100 feet (30m).

WALK 1: KENDAL TO LEVENS BRIDGE AND RETURN

Start: *Miller Bridge, Kendal. Grid Ref 517 927*
Distance: *11¾ miles (19km), climbing 400 feet (120m)*
OS Maps: *English Lakes 1:25,000 (South East) and Pathfinder SD 48/58*
Walking Time: *4 hours*

Three-quarters of this varied walk is, in effect, a linear nature reserve. The outward route follows the course of the River Kent, reputedly the fastest in England, which bisects the silver-grey town, and the return is on the line of the old Lancaster-Kendal canal, some sections of which have been filled in, leaving canal bridges in the middle of fields! Levens Hall (topiary work in the gardens) and Park (with black deer) are additional attractions. Those who wish to walk only half the route can use a handy bus service between Levens Bridge and Kendal.

Kendal, the county town of old Westmorland, is bypassed by the A591. Kendal's one-way traffic system uses Miller Bridge, one of six crossing places of the River Kent. Pressure on adjacent car parking is great, but within easy walking distance are orthodox and multi-storey car parks. The former canal basin, which is five minutes' walk from the bridge, has been levelled and converted into a car park. Crowning a green hill are the ruins of Kendal Castle, commissioned by William Rufus and (in 1543) owned by Thomas Parr, father of Katherine Parr (the luckiest of the wives of Henry VIII in the sense that she outlived him).

From Miller Bridge, stay on the west bank (signposted 'Kirkland via Riverside'), and go in the same direction as the river, almost immediately passing a flood-marker plaque which indicates that in 1898 the depth of water was over man-height. A monument recalls James Cropper, the first MP for Westmorland (a county absorbed in the new Cumbria in 1974). Cropper's paper mill, at Burneside near Kendal, is a major employer in the district. High-rise housing is followed by the elegance of Abbot Hall (art gallery and Museum of Lakeland Life and Industry).

Holy Trinity, Kendal's parish church, stands on the site of a church of Anglian times. The present structure has a grand scale reflective of the boom in the local wool trade. The vast building has five aisles and remnants of three chapels connected with three notable families: Parr, Bellingham and Strickland. Near the Bellingham Chapel are the sword and helmet which belonged to a Royalist, Major Robert Philipson, of Belle Island, Windermere (Robin the Devil). Seeking revenge of Colonel Briggs, a Cromwellian, whom he believed (wrongly) to be in church for a morning service, the galloping major rode into the building, was pulled from his horse by the congregation, and (it is said) re-mounted and was then knocked from his horse while trying to leave by a relatively small door.

At Nether Bridge, keep on the west bank, eventually bearing left at a Chinese restaurant. Do not enter Park Crescent, but swing to the left for the riverside path, which here is flanked by modern housing. Across the Kent is the K Shoes factory shop, which is usually under seige from excursion coaches as well as cars. Our path dips beneath trees to approach the ultramodern Romney Bridge, the successor of a pedestrian suspension bridge, which was moved to a fresh location. At Romney Gardens, and still on the west bank, cross Romney Road (but not the bridge) into

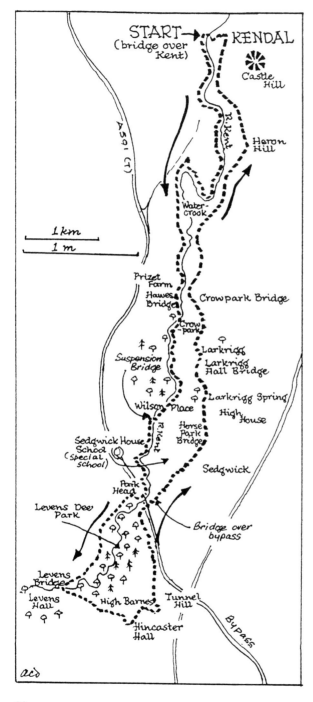

START→ (bridge over Kent)
KENDAL
Castle Hill
R. Kent
A591 (T)
Heron Hill
Water-crook
1 km
1 m
Prizet Farm
Hawes Bridge
Crowpark Bridge
Crow-park
Suspension Bridge
Larkrigg
Larkrigg Hall Bridge
Larkrigg Spring
Wilson Place
High House
Sedgwick House School (Special school)
Horse Park Bridge
R. Kent
Sedgwick
Park Head
Levens Dee Park
Bridge over bypass
Levens Bridge
Levens Hall
High Barnes
Tunnel Hill
Hincaster Hall
Bypass
aco

Ford Terrace and regain the river bank.

Notice that the River Kent has a limestone bed — and the ubiquitous supermarket trolley. The limestone encourages a flush of plant life, and in summer the attention is claimed by meadow cranesbill (a tall plant with large, bright blue-violet petals), ox-eye daisy (large white petals round a yellow centre), knapweed (red-purple flowerheads) and rosebay willow herb (tall, slender, in dense patches, with pink flowers in spike-like clusters). That familiar prickly shrub, gorse, adds a splash of gold when in flower.

The most showy plants are aliens. Parts of the riverbank are clogged by Himalayan balsam, and ragwort cannot be overlooked. Himalayan (or Indian) balsam grows tall and stout-stemmed, putting forth big pinkish purple (sometimes white) flowers. This plant flowers from July to October and, on a hot day, shoots its seeds using a spring mechanism. Ragwort, a native of mountainous areas in southern Europe, introduced to Britain (and the seeds largely spread by being whisked along beside roads and railways), is a plant with clusters of bright yellow flowers showing up well in the summer greenness. Ragwort should be treated with respect. When bruised, it exudes a substance which is poisonous to farmstock. (Further down the Kent is the giant hogweed, which should also be left alone, for its sap can cause skin irritation in humans.)

Opposite a small weir is another K Shoes factory. Soon all traces of urbanisation are left behind. Turn right, then left, following the sinuous course of the Kent. On the opposite bank, where now stands Watercrook (an apt reference to the river) stood a Roman camp named Alavna. A flight of steps connects the riverside walk with a path at higher level. It is attractively backed by houses with floriferous gardens, many with gates giving access to the path. Over a stile, join a minor road, cross a bridge and (at a sign for Hawes Bridge and Prizet) leave the road to follow a field path which leads due south, regaining the riverside at an awkwardly narrow stile.

The River Kent's bank is well wooded, the trees including oak and rowan. Prizet (the large house on the hill to the right) has been converted into flats. The riverside now holds a large number of the showy but sinister giant hogweed, an umbellifer capable of growing to well over eight feet (2.5m). Its white blossom appears in June and July. The stem is stout and hollow. Also plentiful is butterbur. The big, fleshy, heart-shaped leaves (not unlike those of the familiar rhubarb) appear after the flowers. The leaves were once used by farmers' wives for wrapping butter to keep it cool when being taken to Kendal market.

Hawes Bridge spans a limestone ravine where, in normal conditions, the Kent goes white with fury. Here there will be doubt about the next stage, the most prominent path in woodland below the bridge having a 'private' notice. Cross the bridge to the east bank. An unmarked step–stile gives access to a faint field path. It runs beside woodland, above the ravine, towards Sedgwick. As the river widens, Robin Hoods Island is seen. Plants beside the path include meadowsweet, pink campion, harebell and St Johns wort.

At Wilson Place is a 'talking' suspension bridge (listen to it as you cross). Bear left onto tarmac, dodging cars and caravans associated with the Low Park Wood site. At a T-junction, resist (if you can) the temptations of the Strickland Arms, half a mile away (0.8km) to the right. Go straight ahead to a second junction, go left, ignore the river bridge and continue on a cul-de-sac which passes cottages overlooking a stretch of the Kent with much outcropping rock, some of it chipped away to help migratory fish — salmon and sea trout. Their up–river passage varies according to the state of the river, but is usually in early autumn.

The path becomes curiouser and curiouser, at one stage clinging beneath a concrete bridge (part of the Kendal bypass) and continuing on a route signed Levens Bridge. On the left is a tall wall, topped by wire, which marks the periphery of the deer park, a private park associated with Levens Estate, owned for many years by the Bagot family. The park is entered by way of a substantial stile, and a public right of way across the broad grassland is waymarked.

Look for medium–sized deer which, being chocolate-brown on the upper body and of a buffish tone lower down and on the legs, are dark-phase fallow deer which have been here for centuries. The males have horns and are called bucks; the females are does. In summer the spade-antlers of the bucks are forming behind a hairy skin called 'velvet'. Also in the park are Bagot goats, one of the 'rare breeds'.

At Levens Bridge, you will reach the A6 road near a lofty wall, above which appear the roofscapes of Levens Hall and other buildings. Levens Hall, open to view at prescribed times, began life in 1300 as a pele tower, used for defence. To the writer Mrs Humphrey Ward in 1897 it was 'the wonderful grey house' with a topiary garden like nothing else, with 'broad straight, gravelled paths among the fantastic creatures &

The topiary gardens at Levens Hall date from the end of the seventeenth century.

pyramids & crowns'. Today, Levens is the proverbial 'must' for those who love historic gardens. They are usually open daily. The gardening design, with much topiary work, is unchanged since Monsieur Beaumont created them, beginning in 1690. He worked at Levens until his death, forty years later.

The return to Kendal begins by crossing the main road bridge to the second signpost, marked Hincaster, between the bridge and the bus shelter. Where open farmland is reached, an impressive section of the park wall is seen (left) and not infrequently Bagot goats will be in view beyond it. Our route climbs to High Barns, which has all the grace and beauty of Levens, a further sign for Hincaster offering reassurance. In the field beyond, a large herd of Friesian cattle (black and white) might be assembling for milking. At the top gate, join a clear track to Hincaster Hall, a private house which is seen (below left) after topping a rise. Follow

the track to the right of the hall down a minor road to Hincaster village.

You are about to enter the strange, almost lost world of the canal which linked the navigable lower Lune with Kendal. On reaching Hincaster, a sign marked Well Heads is seen. The inclination is to go straight ahead, climbing on a well-trodden but overgrown path. Ignore that track, which was the one used by canal horses which, in the absence of a towpath, could not use the Hincaster Tunnel. To the left of the sign for Well Heads is a property known as the Barns. Our path runs to the rear of it, in junglish conditions, emerging on the canal towpath, in an area which is gloriously overgrown.

To the right, and a few paces away, is the tunnel mouth. (At the start of the next stage, the walker may look back and see light at the far end.) Hincaster Canal Tunnel is 378 yards (345m) long, 76 feet (23m) below the summit of the hill and 146 feet (45m) above sea level. An impressive feature of a waterway built in 1816-17, it was last used locally in 1944. With no towpath within the tunnel, barges were either pulled through by rope or 'legged', the men lying on the barge and 'walking' on the side walls of the tunnel.

Jungle conditions prevail in summer, when the sunlight slants between gaps in a canopy of leaves. The bed of the canal is clear to see. Some stretches hold a little water; others are damp and overgrown. The trees include alder, which grows in moist places. Bullrushes have set themselves in the damp mud. The path is easy to follow, terminating against a fence bordering the A590, which is here in a deep cutting. Retrace your steps for about fifty yards (45m) where there is a gap leading on to a minor road which eventually arrives at the edge of Levens Park. An avenue of beech trees forms what looks like an aisle in some gloomy old cathedral. The road crosses the A590. Look out for a flight of steps leading back to the course of the canal. Of the canal itself there is not a trace, the land having been infilled to provide pasturage for sheep and beef stock. Follow the contour and a track materialises. Sedgwick House, with its prominent tower and clock, is visible to the left. The house is now a special school. Pass under the arch of a canal bridge which is an incongruous feature of the field.

Beyond, the bed of the canal is visible, and alongside it a well-used path from which you look down on the roofs of Sedgwick village (connected by steps; the village has a store). Canal Trust volunteeers keep the path well-mown, and its fences and stiles in good condition. Beyond the village, all trace of the canal is lost beyond a gate, on the reverse of which are the words: 'The Wharf; please keep to the footpath'. Sequestered by trees, Horse Park Bridge is another which now stands in the middle of

A preserved bridge in a curious location, along a filled-in stretch of the Lancaster–Kendal Canal.

nowhere. Beyond is Larkrigg Wood, with strong evidence of the canal bed.

Leaving the wood, the outward course is below and left. The outskirts of Kendal are reached after first crossing the Natland road. Follow the signs for 'Canal Head' — and beware of cyclists, who also have right of access to the path. Take care when crossing the Endmoor road. The large building on the left is Kendal's sports centre (with car park, swimming pool and café). The path, broad and firm, takes the walker unerringly, via a Norweb depot and light industrial works, to Canal Head.

The head of the former basin is adjacent to the grandly titled 'civic amenity site' — a public refuse disposal point, from where a road leads between the premises of Samuel Gawith & Co Ltd, snuffmakers since 1792, and Gilbert Gilkes & Gordon Ltd, whose products (water turbines and pumps) are in use worldwide. Miller Bridge, our starting point, is near at hand.

WALK 2: SCOUT SCAR AND CUNSWICK SCAR

Start: *Kendal Town Hall.* Grid Ref: *515 926*
Distance: *7 miles (11km), climbing 1,000 feet (300m)*
OS Map: *English Lakes 1:25,000 (South East)*
Time: *4½ hours*

This is the right royal route which every able-bodied visitor staying in or around Kendal should take as an introduction to the area. From the town, the route sweeps up grandly to a range of limestone scars which are natural vantage points for most of the Lakeland peaks. On the descent, the way passes through woodland to Fellside at Kendal, where the houses huddle closely together as though for mutual comfort. Kendal is now bypassed by the A591. The town centre is subject to a one-way traffic system. Car parks are well marked. You may find yourself in a street where parking is handy — and free.

Kendal, which prospered mightily from the fourteenth century through the wool trade, now has industrial diversion but contrives to keep its populace busy. K Shoes take their name from the initial letter of the town. A world-famous builder of turbines was referred to by W H Auden in a prose-poem, in which a lover is described as 'more beautiful than a badger, a sea-horse or a turbine built by Gilkes & Co of Kendal'. The town grew up by the Kent (anciently known as Can). The shell of the thirteenth century Kendal Castle may be visited. In the seventeenth century, the Kings Arms specialised in potted char, a fish caught in Windermere and some other lakes. Arthur Young (visiting the same inn in 1768) varied his consumption of potted char with 'a brace of woodcocks, veal cutlets and cheese, one shilling a head, dinner'.

Kendal Town Hall, on its present site, dates from 1858, and in 1894 the building was enlarged at the expense of Alderman and Mrs Bindloss. They also covered the cost of the clock tower and its carillon. The alderman, when in his sixth year of office as mayor (1895), died without seeing the project completed. His name is commemorated by that of one of the rooms. The carillon plays a different tune, at three hour intervals, during each day of the week but is silent at night. From the town hall, cross the road at the traffic lights to Allhallows Lane, which ascends to Beast Banks, on the right-hand side of which, the former national school for boys has been impressively renovated and converted into housing. Across Beast Banks may be seen the door leading to the Scotch Burial Ground (1760-1855). It is not the final resting place of a cache of whisky.

Where the road forks, stay on the left lower leg which has a sign indicating 'Scout Scar'. On the left is the old Inghamite chapel, rebuilt in 1844. The road climbs steadily to cross the Kendal bypass, beyond which the first path for Scout Scar, at a once impressive gateway, should be ignored in favour of another path, a hundred yards (90m) beyond and just outside the Kendal boundary. The stile is a tight fit. Beyond, the path bisects the former (and still discernible) Kendal racecourse, and beyond it another constricted gate, this time of the 'kissing' variety. A ragged landscape is dotted with juniper. The foliage is prickly. Crush it and you detect a tang of apples. Three years elapse before the fruit, having gone from green to dark blue, ripens and becomes black.

This approach to Scout Scar is not sour land. Limestone obtrudes, with the visible rock fragmented. The route is clear to see, and after a long mile (1.6km) descends gently to a cairn on Scout Scar, which properly is the name of the southern end of Underbarrow Scar and is one of the two guardian limestone hills of the Lyth Valley. The other is Whitbarrow (*walk 13*), to the south-west. Immediately below Scout Scar is Barrowfield Farm. Much of this escarpment, and adjacent Cunswick Scar, form a Site of Special Scientific Interest (SSSI). In spring, cowslip and rock rose are to be found, also several varieties of orchid, including early purple. Dark red helliborine has been recorded. Birds-foot trefoil, wild thyme and dropwort testify to the sweetness imparted by the limestone.

The long escarpment which takes in Scout Scar and Cunswick Scar has a good range of the more colourful plants. They include horseshoe vetch and rock rose (yellow), flowering in May and June, and bloody cranesbill (crimson-purple), flowering June to August. Also growing in the area, but not as noticeable as the trio just mentioned, is mountain everlasting, which forms a mat on the ground and produces a mass of whitish or pinkish flower-heads.

Of the birdlife, kestrel and raven are regularly seen. A kestrel has a plumage of rufous chestnut, the male having a blue-grey head and tail. The kestrel's food-hunting routine of maintaining a fixed position in the sky as it scans the ground is familiar to anyone who has driven along a motorway, much less trodden rough paths in wild places. A skylark has an affinity with the kestrel in its ability to maintain a position high above the ground, where it is like a feathered helicopter. Green woodpecker might be seen feeding on the ground

The relatively large yellow flowers of rock rose emerge in May and June. It occurs in limestone terrain, such as the Site of Special Scientific Interest which includes parts of Scout Scar and Cunswick Scar.

where ants are numerous. In autumn, flocks of Scandinavian thrushes (fieldfares with some redwings) dine on the thorn berries. The fieldfares are distinctive because these thrushes have a plumage patched with grey and coarse chacking voices.

Turn right to walk due north along the edge of Scout Scar. Take care, especially

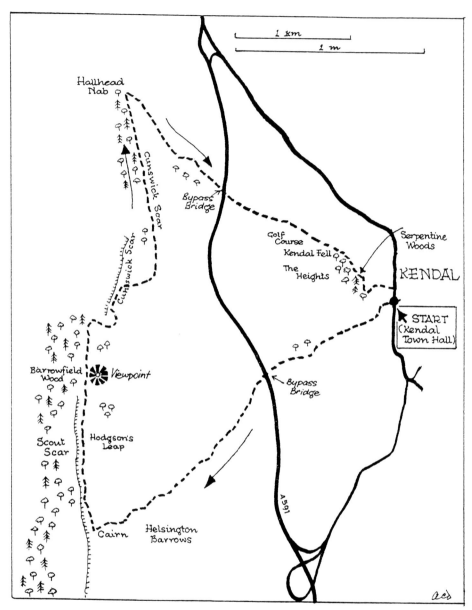

in wet conditions, limestone lacking adhesion and the ground falling away as near vertical as makes no difference. Set back from the edge is the aptly-named Mushroom, a structure occupying the site of a

mountain indicator and shelter first constructed in 1912 as a memorial to George V, and marking the summit at 764 feet (233m). The rim of the roof is marked out to indicate special features of the panoramic view. Back at the scar edge, you will see Barrowfield Wood, with a fair sprinkling of silver birch which in winter takes on a purple hue. A few sturdy Scots pine, the upper bark peeling to reveal an orange shade, contrast with the other woodland species of tree. The track swings (right) and descends to the road which lies between the two scars.

Across the road, and immediately beyond a quarry car park, follow a narrow path which climbs steeply but after only twenty yards (18m) swings left to contour the rim, using a permissive path to the west of a police radio tower. Pass through a copse to a wall corner, where a step-stile becames visible at the last moment and a sign indicates Cunswick Fell. The way is now clear, and beyond a crossing of paths swings left on to Cunswick Scar, the line of which is further east than Scout Scar. Follow the length of Cunswick Scar for one mile (1.6km) to Hallhead Nab, thence, with the ground dropping away northwards, to an area with an extensive view — the Kentmere Valley and the Far Eastern Fells of Lakeland. In prominent view, north-east, is the paper mill complex of Croppers of Burneside.

At Hallhead Nab, where a track continues north for Burneside, instead double back to your right, climbing to the summit cairn on Cunswick Scar at 679 feet (207m). Aim next for a copse on the skyline, south-south-east, the path becoming clearer at the approach to a limestone wall, which is straddled by a step-stile. The limestone walls and verdant grassland associated with limestone provide enjoyable walking country. At this point, the Kendal bypass runs in a limestone cutting, which muffles the sound. Safely across the footbridge,

ignore the paths heading left and right, continuing ahead, to cross the Kendal golf course. The sheep of this area include a proportion of the traditional local breed, Kendal Roughs (Rough Fells), which thrive on the dry slaty fells of what used to be Westmorland.

The path over the golf course is clearly marked. The initials GUR indicates 'ground under repair' and should be avoided. Kendal is soon in view. The town centre is dominated by the premises of Provincial Assurance. Leave the golf course through a narrow stile, traversing the fellside and passing a stand of pines. Ahead are Serpentine Woods, in which you should keep to the stepped path descending (left). A tree trunk with the outline of a butterfly carved into it is part of an alphabetic nature trail laid by the Kendal branch of the Cumbria Wildlife Trust many years ago. The letter C was represented by a carving of a caterpillar which was stolen. There are plans to renew this extensive trail.

Emerge on to the tarmac opposite a sign 'Hallsfell Nab 1', within yards turning right into Queens Road. At the first acute junction, descend the cobbled steps of Fell Brow, swinging right at the bottom on to Church Terrace, at the rear of the attractive All Hallows Church, thence crossing the Syke on to Middle Lane in front of the same church! Next go down more steps to cross Low Fell Side. Another flight of steps takes the form of ribbed cobbles, on which care is needed when they are wet. They lead to a snicket at the rear of Martindale Builders before emerging from Entry Lane on to Stricklandgate. Turn right to return to the town hall.

WALK 3: THE RIVER SPRINT AND POTTER FELL

Start: *Staveley. Grid Ref: 470 983*
Distance: *8½ miles (13.5km), climbing 900 feet (275m)*
OS Map: *English Lakes 1:25,000 (South East)*
Walking Time: *5½ hours*

This walk falls into three contrasting sections. Firstly, a riverside stretch close to the banks of the River Kent, in part using the Dales Way (Ilkley-Bowness), passing through an area where paper-making began about 1760 when Thomas Ashburner built the Cowen Head Mill. Then a long ascent, initially by the River Sprint. Finally, a moorland crossing over Potter Fell, which is owned by the Cropper family, papermakers of Burneside, who celebrated 150 years in business in 1995. The fell is notable for its tarns. Staveley, bypassed by the A591, has car parking places, with shops and inns to hand.

Staveley, beside the old route from Kendal to Windermere, is a long-drawn-out village. A curiosity is that the church and tower are on opposite sides of the road. Discerning walkers know Staveley as the access point for Kentmere and its majestic horseshoe of fells. Using Staveley as a starting point, you may explore a man-made landscape of considerable interest. Start beside the Duke William pub in Main Street and take an enclosed path between this and the churchyard and tower of St Margarets Church. Pass the bowling green before using an attractive footbridge across the Kent. Turn right. Where the path forks, continue ahead through a kissing-gate.

Half-left is a cluster of farm buildings, an arrow giving direction between them, and beyond a desirable property,

Grouse are found where there is a covering of heather, such as on Potter Fell, as heather is their main source of food. It is the cock bird who has the shiny reddish-brown plumage and red eye-wattles.

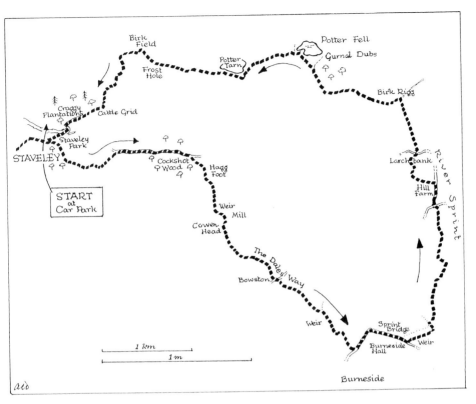

Birk
Field

Potter Fell

Gurnal Dubs

Potter
Tarn

Frost
Hole

Birk Rigg

Craggy
Plantations

Cattle Grid

Staveley
Park

STAVELEY

Cockshot
Wood

Hagg
Foot

Larch bank

Hill
Farm

START
at
Car Park

Weir

Mill

Cowen
Head

The Dales Way

Bowston

Weir

Sprint
Bridge

Burneside
Hall

Weir

1 km

1 m

Burneside

ac̀ò

follow a tractor-way under a canopy of trees until, at a further kissing-gate, our track strikes off left. Aim for a line of hawthorns, from where a step-stile will be seen. The path momentarily rejoins the riverbank before emerging on the back lane linking Staveley with Bowston, adjacent to the local sewage works. The scene is mitigated, in late summer and into autumn, by a vast display of devils-bit scabious, a tall perennial with blue-purple flowers on long-stalked heads.

Follow the road (right) for a long third of a mile (0.5km) until, after crossing a stream, you see a path (right) into decid-uous woodland, including much oak, which is managed by a conservation body, the Woodland Trust. Sessile is the type of oak common in the Lake District, it being a tree of the hillside as opposed to the valley,

named 'sessile' because the acorns do not have stalks. Ignore a track from Hagg Foot, which crosses the one you are following; and also avoid crossing the river. The weir at Cowen Head is seen, and near it is a complex of luxury apartments which have been so well designed they blend into the natural rock-scape where the river enters a ravine.

You have reached the site of the old Cowen Head Mills, once part of the James Cropper paper-making enterprise, all of which is now based at Burneside, 1¼ miles (2km) downstream. A golf course is being developed. Years ago, industrialised Cowen Head was linked with Burneside by stand-ard gauge railway, its course being traceable between Bowston, your next call, and Burne-side. The footpath follows a level course and the road undulates. Continue beside the

41

river, passing Bowston to reach the outskirts of Burneside, an Old English name meaning 'Brunulf's hill'. A recent diversion of the path further north has allowed the factory to be extended. The mill race, weir and salmon-ladder associated with Croppers, a much-respected local firm, are seen before you follow the diverted stretch under the inscrutable gaze of security cameras. Trees have been planted to provide natural cover.

Joining a road, turn left to pass Burneside Hall, which has a duck-haunted pond. At a road junction, go right, then cross Sprint Bridge, immediately following the path (left). The Sprint, vying with the Kent in a claim to be the swiftest river in England, rises in the shadow of Gatesgarth Pass, at the head of Longsleddale, and drains the whole of that valley before joining the Kent ten miles (16km) and 1,200 feet (365m) lower down. Cross the bridge to Sprint Mill Cottages, passing beneath a bower before swinging right (ignore the gate) and taking the path to the topside of this. The river is crossed by the Thirlmere-Manchester pipeline, an astonishing engineering feat, the water supply being worked throughout by gravity.

The Sprint swirls through rocky pools and on its bank is a picnic spot, with slate seats and matching table. These clear, cool, fast-flowing rivers attract the dipper, a plump little bird which exploits a niche of its own, feeding on creatures which it locates around the rocks. The river swings away, right, and the course you take is now due north, crossing several fields with just one arrow to reassure you that this is indeed a right of way, there being no path visible. A minor lane is gained at a junction.

Continue ahead on the lane, passing Hill Farm and, 70 yards (65m) further, veering left at the neighbouring Hill Fold. Leave this through a gateway into a pasture, where high-tension electricity wires give a rough indication of the course of the path. Aim

for Larchbank, the highest of a clutch of buildings ahead. A step-stile will be found at the field corner, permitting access to a rough track. From Larchbank are grand views down the Kent Valley. The gardens are immaculately maintained.

Up the drive, follow the arrow through an unusual step-stile which incorporates its own gate. Incline to the right to join and cross a lane. Beyond, climbing begins in earnest to a rough track serving the fell tarns. Stop to take in the view (and gain fresh breath). To your left is the ridge of Whinfell and to the right is Cunswick Scar. A feature to the east is the A6, backed by the Howgill Fells, Garsdale, the Kent Valley and Kendal. The track goes left and passes, as it climbs, the site of dried-up Low Taggleshaw.

This little-known hill country of old Westmorland consists of low, rounded hills and ridges, some of which are empurpled in late summer by the flowering of bell heather and ling. You may hear the crowing of the cock grouse or even see a covey of grouse in flight. If a grouse is seen on the ground, notice it is a stubby bird with rust-coloured plumage and white feathers to the legs, like avian spats. The grouse are restricted to the heather moor because most of their food is the tough, fibrous heather. Old heather is burnt off by gamekeepers to encourage the growth of new shoots. Grouse chicks need the nourishment of a large and varied insect life, so they are taken to those soft patches on a moor where sphagnum moss grows. In moist areas grows the alluring grass of Parnassus, a hairless perennial which boasts several flowering stems holding pale flowers, with large petals on which are conspicuous veins.

Round a bend lies Gurnal Dubs, the most attractive of the tarns of Potter Fell. The tarn is served by paths both to the north and south, the former being the most attractive. With its fringe of vegetation, this

Gurnal Dubs was one of a number of tarns created artificially on Potter Fell to provide a regular supply of water for the Cropper paper mills, based to the south of here at Burneside.

tarn is the nesting place of great crested grebe. Look for a moderately large bird which swims low in the water but has a long white neck. Feathers at the neck were once in great demand for women's fashion and this grebe was hunted. Numbers have now recovered and pairs breed on most large stretches of water. It is unusual to find a pair on a high tarn.

At Gurnal Dubs, a boathouse lies close to the dam, and from here a clear track heads east over initially rising ground before crossing a causeway — an earlier dam — and arrives at Potter Tarn, where drystone walls, plunging into the water, betray its artificial nature. A spring emerges from the bed of the watercourse below the dam. Each tarn supplies water to the paper mills. Continue west to a wall stile, from where

the route is waymarked, continuing down to a track with a sign indicating there is no right of way for walkers. Pass through a gate opposite, leading down to a stream and marshy ground (left). An enclosed path leads unexpectedly by right of way through the environs of Birk Field, presently let as holiday accommodation. At the far gate, ascend the metalled lane to emerge on the loop road.

There is a choice now of either the road veering left or a footpath via Piked Howe. It matters little, the two meeting five minutes later. Beyond Craggypark Plantation, the valley road is met but briefly, leaving by alternative path descending through Staveley Park to rejoin the outward route close to the footbridge over the River Kent. The bar of the Duke William now beckons.

WALK 4: TWIXT KENT AND SPRINT

Start:	*Ullthwaite Bridge. Grid Ref: 455 012*
Distance:	*9 miles (14.5km), climbing 1,000 feet (300m)*
OS Map:	*1:25,000 English Lakes (South East)*
Time:	*5 hours*

Lying between the familiar dales of the Lake District are wide tracts of little-known country. This is borne out by a traverse between Kentmere (River Kent) and Longsleddale (River Sprint). The fells forming this area are visible from the Kendal bypass by northward-bound travellers, one of whom compared the group with a giant caterpillar. Chose a clear day, to enjoy the views from unexpected locations and because the somewhat featureless plateau may cause confusion in mist. A compass may be useful. The bridleway linking the two is, for the most part, clear underfoot. The last stage of the walk, back in Kentmere, passes historic Kentmere Hall and bird-busy Kentmere. Allow a further one and a quarter hours for optional excursions to the summit of Green Quarter Fell and Skeggles Water.

Initially, approach Kentmere from Staveley, now bypassed by the A591. There is parking for three vehicles near Ullthwaite Bridge, some two miles (3km) along the minor road leading from the village. Dorothy Wordsworth and her brother William visited Staveley in 1794, 'when we first began our pilgrimage together'. They drank 'a bason of milk at a publick house' and Dorothy 'washed my feet in the brook and put on a pair of silk stockings by Wm's advice'.

Lower Kentmere is rich in old woodland, where one of the appealing local birds is a summer visitor, the pied flycatcher. The cock bird has a handsome pied plumage. Like all flycatchers, the pied catches insects by leaping out at them from a perch. From where the car has been parked, follow the road northwards for 300 yards (270m) to a plantation (right), where a bridleway for Longsleddale climbs steeply through a larch wood. Felling has been taking place on the higher slope; a rough count of the 'rings' on a larch stump indicating that the trees had been planted sixty-five years ago.

On reaching open ground, do not be tempted to follow the wall (left) flanking Philipsons Wood. Our course swings right, changing direction from north-east to south-east and heading for a gate on the skyline. The gradient eases at a plateau, where a north-east course is resumed. Follow the wall (right) while admiring the view into upper Kentmere, where the church dominates the mid-ground. Rough country to its left leads to Yoke, just topped by Ill Bell. High Street forms the backdrop. Mardale Ill Bell dips to Nan Bield Pass. The sweep of high fells is completed by Harter Fell, Kentmere Pike and Shipman Knotts.

The landscape through which our route passes has dry hummocks tufty with *Nardus stricta*. This is 'white moor'. Wainwright, in a reference to Green Quarter Fell, called it a 'featureless grassy height'. The lower ground tends to be marshy, with expanses of sphagnum moss. In spring, the sky is busy with skylarks. This species is relatively small, streaky-brown and with a longish tail, the outer feathers being white. The energy of the bird in flying like a feathered helicopter and giving a sustained song is astonishing.

Into view comes an area preserved as heather moor because of anti-sheep walls and the burning of rank old heather to encourage the growth of fresh shoots. The

Green Quarter Fell stretches across the upland between the rivers Kent and Sprint.

outflow from Skeggles Water is seen long before the lake itself comes into view. The flow of water is so strong, it sustains the dipper, a chocolate-brown bird (looking black from a distance) with a bold white 'bib' and a habit of bobbing while standing on a stone. The dipper's call is a metallic *zit, zit zit.*

Continue through two gates. Skeggleswater Dike is to the right. Where the track forks, go left, gaining height, and with a sheepfold (left). Reaching a further plateau, high fells to the east of Longsleddale are seen. They include Tarn Crag and Grey Crag. Directly ahead is a substantial hut in a sheltered hollow on Green Quarter Fell, but our course takes us close to a ruined barn, not far from where a track from Kentmere joins the major inter-dale track. Twisted hawthorns tell of climatic savagery.

Hollow Moor, 1,394 feet (426m), the 'attic' of the wide-spreading Green Quarter

Fell, is close at hand and might be bagged. It is worth climbing if only to bring Skeggles Water (named after a Norseman called Skakull) into view, about a quarter of a mile (0.4km) to the east. A clear path leads to the lake, which has kept its lonely atmosphere. Some years ago, there was a proposal to take diatomite from Skeggles Water, but a howl of protest went up from preservationists and local people. The plan was then dropped. Most of the sheep in this coarse grassland are Rough Fells, originally bred for the dry, slaty Howgills and other austere Westmorland fells.

Back on the original track, contour Cocklaw Fell, which is frequented by fell ponies. They may give the impression of being wild, but each one has a legal owner. Longsleddale opens up. Just beyond a cross-wall is a good spot for lunch. A path descends (right) by way of Tills Hole to Sadgill. Those who yearn for an immediate return

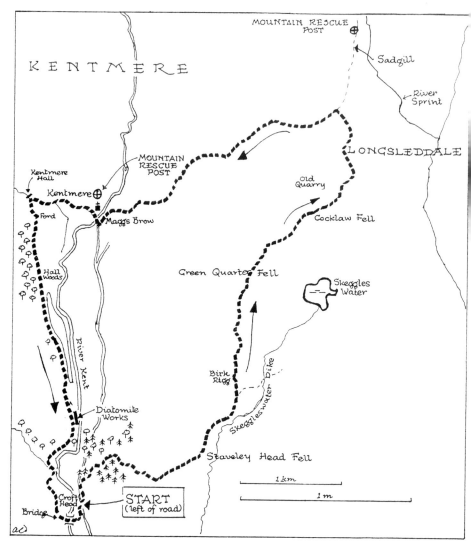

to Kentmere should continue along the contour, beside a line of trees, to meet the Sadgill-Kentmere track. Go left up a steep but stepped course. At the col, a wall is breached by a stile and a gate. Opt for the former, the more direct course for Kentmere, which is entered by a series of zigzags. Reaching tarmac, a sign announces 'Maggs Brow, B & B, evening meals and teas', a worthy enterprise, with a choice of venue, either indoors (the Dipping Shed) or on a terrace, from which there is a stimulating view. One of the adornments is a mossy pair of walking boots, filled with soil and now serving as plant pots.

Swing right for Brockstones, Hollow Bank and Overend at the T-junction. A footpath sign indicates a path which descends through a stand of larch to rejoin the road lower down. At Low Bridge, bear right for Kentmere Church, which is dedicated to St Cuthbert and has sixteenth century roof-beams. Notice how the land to the south of the church is almost as flat as a bowling green. Once it formed the head of the great mere of the Kent. The infilling process began at the time of its creation. Stones and mud were washed down from the fells, peat formed at a particularly wet period and the deposition of diatomite occurred. These are formed from the skeleton of diatoms (tiny plants).

Leave the road in front of the church in favour of a metalled track bound for Kentmere Hall (not open to the public), former home of the de Gilpin family. It has a fourteenth century pele tower as its core, a rare instance of such a tower built in an upper dale and possibly related, by its defensive nature, to the once-important Penrith-Kendal route via Mardale and Nan Bield Pass. The dwelling attached to Kentmere Hall was replaced on a bigger scale in the more settled days of the sixteenth century. A vague folk memory credits Richard Gilpin with the death of the last wild boar in England. The most famous of the local Gilpins was Bernard, born at Kentmere Hall in 1517. He became Archdeacon of Durham and, being a great champion of the Reformation, was dubbed the Apostle of the North.

Pass through the farmyard to take the footpath (first left), an easy track fringing Hall Woods before climbing slightly to parallel all that remains of the once extensive mere of the Kent. Now enter an industrial complex, the diatomite works of Hepworth Minerals and Chemicals Ltd. For many years, diatomous earth has been dredged from Waterfoot (the foot of the old Kent Mere) to provide first-rate insulation material for the building trade. A centuries-old wooden boat, recovered from the bed of the mere in 1955, was presented to the National Maritime Museum.

From the motor road across the valley, there is the slightest glint of open water, but from the nearby path it is seen to be quite extensive and the haunt of waterfowl, including goldeneye in winter. Harriet Martineau wrote in 1854 of the old Kentmere Tarn that 'it is drained away; and fertile fields now occupy the place of the swamp, reeds and shallow water...'

Leave by the gate marked 'Pottery. 15mph.' There is no sign of a pottery, much less of crockery travelling at speed. Sawmill Cottage sits in an idyllic spot at the confluence of Park Beck and the River Kent. A path flanked by iron railings leads to a crossing of the former before becoming enclosed by high walls. At the T-junction, swing left to follow a deer fence protecting newly-planted saplings. Beyond Croft Head and Ullthwaite, cross the Kent to return to the valley road exactly where you left your transport a few hours earlier.

WALK 5: THE SOURCE OF THE RIVER KENT

Start: *Kentmere Church. Grid Ref 456 041*
Distance: *7½ miles (12km), climbing 650 feet (200m)*
OS Map: *English Lakes 1:25,000 (South East)*
Walking Time: *4 hours*

Water gushing from some of Lakeland's shapeliest fells — Ill Bell, Froswick, High Street and Lingmell End — converges in Hall Cove and creates the Kent, the swiftest river in England (though claims are made for the nearby Sprint). The topmost reach of Kentmere has much evidence of our industrial past. A reservoir regulated the river for the benefit of about ninety water-powered mills lower down. On either side of the valley are disused slate workings which demonstrate the energy and ingenuity of 't' owd man', as past generations of workers are collectively known. To reach Kentmere, follow the A591 Kendal bypass, then go on for a mile or two and turn off along the minor road through Staveley.

Mention has already been made of Dorothy Wordsworth's impression of Staveley (*walk 4*), but she was being a little extravagant with words when she called it 'a mountain village'. It is, however, an attractive little village, and from it a narrow winding road is followed to its termination near Kentmere Church. Parking becomes ever more difficult in upper Kentmere. A bus service from Kendal provides a summer service. Sometimes, parking in a field near Low Bridge is available at a reasonable charge. An alternative start for those with their own transport is to take the road which branches (right) before Low Bridge and follow it to near Brockstones, where there is limited parking near the start of a bridleway to Sadgill.

The walk to Kentmere reservoir is easy, on clear paths almost all the way. The return from the head of the valley is not quite so straightforward. The infant Kent must be forded, to the north of the reservoir, which may be tricky in very wet weather. A footbridge would be of help here. The area abounds with interest and is suitable for most weather conditions, even when the tops of the fells are gale-wracked.

Facing Kentmere Church at the start of the walk, take the public footpath to the right of the building. The route is initially tarmaced and heads northwards. Where it forks, opt for the high road, which provides the best views. Within a few minutes, the two routes rejoin at Rook Howe. An awesome sight is provided by huge boulders in the fields or having been incorporated in walls. It is an area of sheep and a few beef cattle of mixed parenthood, but with some showing the white faces of Herefords.

A step-stile (right) leads to a crossing of the Kent (used during the return from walk 6). Your course is ahead, to where a way-mark indicates a step-stile over a minor beck, thence over soggy ground on our way to rougher country. At Calfhowe Crag, pass through a gate and go right to join a vehicular route serving two farms and the former quarries. The first farm, Scales, overlooks a valley bottom, contrasting starkly with the increasing grandeur around. Next is Hart-rigg, an imposing Victorian set-up in a small-dale setting. Holding pens for farm stock make clever use of the landforms. One is concreted, though at an acute angle. The farmstead is sheltered from the bitterest winds by tall trees over which a buzzard might be circling. The kestrel, another brownish bird but smaller, demonstrates its

48

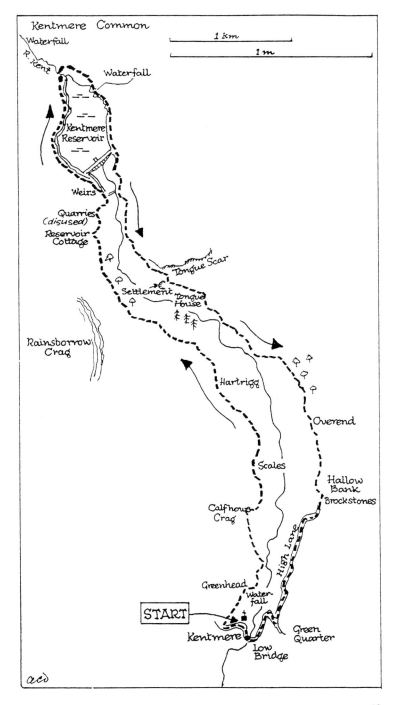

The scattered village of Kentmere has a majestic setting. The austere Church of St Cuthbert has sixteenth century roof-beams, but was restored during the nineteenth century.

distinctive hunting tactic — hovering on the wind, scanning the ground, then diving quickly and silently to collect some luckless mouse or vole.

Beyond this farm, the track leaves tarmac to climb and meander, questing for higher ground. The head of Kentmere is dramatically revealed. Experimental enclosures on either side of the path hold saplings of indigenous species, with fencing to protect them from hungry sheep, if not

from deer, which sometimes include outlying red stags from the Martindale area to the north. Red deer have a 'plastic' quality; their size varies, according to the terrain. At least three types of red deer are to be found in Lakeland, which is only thirty miles (50km) across. The Martindale animals, reared and living their lives on open fells, are the most impoverished. It is more than likely that you will see a raven, attention being drawn to it by its hoarse call. The wheatear, a summer bird visitor, is drawn to such a rocky landscape and usually nests in a disused rabbit burrow. Small and lively, the cock wheatear impresses by its smart plumage of French grey. Roe deer and red squirrels might be encountered in wooded areas much lower down the valley.

Below Rainsborrow Crag (left) and also high on the fell are spoil heaps backed by two large man-made caves. Some quarry buildings have been sympathetically adapted to new uses. A gable wall has been bitumised against the winter easterlies. Splendid new slate walls enclose an area through which a stream has been covered with large slates.

Now the reaches of the Kent are in view. This river is home to the white-clawed crayfish. (A rarer species, the one-clawed white crayfish, took exception to a naturalist visitor, giving her a nasty nip.) The 'white-clawed' prefix was given to distinguish our native crayfish from the American variety which, being larger and more aggressive, is taking over in some northwestern rivers. To find a crayfish, simply turn over some of the stones in the beck.

A brief sortie might be made into the nearest quarry, a gaping chasm being enough to deter further exploration. The quarry is a good place to shelter in wild weather, with an abundance of ready-made picnic tables for more favourable conditions. Rejoin the main track by crossing the level top of the spoil heap. Around the next corner is the greater of the Kentmere reservoir spillways, now overgrown. The dam,

A grand accompaniment of fells encircle the head of Kentmere and offer ever-changing views of it, such as from the Ill Bell Ridge. The infant River Kent is seen entering Kentmere left of centre, whilst Lingmell End protrudes from Mardale Ill Bell.

built in 1845, is larger than you might imagine, if you have only seen it only from the Nan Bield path (*walk 6*). Now that it is in need of repair, what had been an expanse of water is now mud and weed. Harriet Martineau, of Ambleside, writing of Kentmere in 1854, and noting that Kentmere Tarn — the natural mere, below the village — had been drained, wrote:

While this tarn existed, the mills at Kendal were but very irregularly supplied with water. Now, when the streams are collected in a reservoir ... and the intercepting tarn is done away with, the flow of water no longer fails.

A survey is being undertaken for Croppers of Burneside, the owners, to assess what must be done.

A thin path, barely discernible at its northern extremity, skirts the west side of the reservoir to climb into Hall Cove. Over your left shoulder is the formidable northeast ridge of Ill Bell, which is marginally less severe than the north face of the Eiger. Clockwise, look at Froswick and High Street, with Lingmell's dramatic spur protruding at the head of the reservoir. East of the valley is the sprawling mass of Kentmere Pike.

As already mentioned, patience must be exercised to find a good place to cross in times of spate. Safely (if not necessarily dryshod), follow the east bank to the reservoir near a solitary old larch. There is no path. The easiest course is to climb through one of the many gaps in the wall and follow the course of the floodbank, where a path will be found. As the dam is reached, a second spillway, much smaller than the last, is crossed to meet a well-worn path down the valley.

Across the Kent, at a lower level, is a sheepfold with a smaller fold on ground sloping towards the water. Almost certainly this complex was used in the days when the fell sheep were washed to remove dirt and impurities from the fleeces about a fortnight before clipping time. Contour a spoil heap and, if feeling adventurous, enter a former quarry (left) and climb (with a clinking of slate underfoot) a slope to find the entrance to a level in which slate was quarried. It extends into Tongue Scar, access being prevented by a substantial grille. Especially noticeable on a cold winter day is the blast of warm air emanating from the enormous hole. Walk across the spoil heap and descend to regain the path by an easy gradient.

As the walk progresses, the ruins of Tongue House are passed. The track from Nan Bield (*used on walk 6*) is seen (left) at a higher level; the two routes do not meet until reaching Overend, half a mile (0.8km) further on. A choice of routes is presented. The high road is preferable, affording good views and also the negotiation of a stockyard astride the road. Gates have to be opened — and closed again. Near Hollow Bank, a bridleway goes right. Ignore this and, still descending, reach the well-known route into Longsleddale. Stay on tarmac, descending through an impressive cutting between drystone walls which must be eight feet (2.5m) high, having three rows of 'throughs'.

Turn sharp right, opposite a sign which (if it has survived) reads: 'Teas, soft drinks; B & B. If in I'm open til 7pm.' At the bottom of the hill, near Low Bridge, turn right to regain the road, returning to the church. It is said that when the Kentmere reservoir was being made, Irish labour was used, and much whisky and ale were sipped at an inn which stood near Low Bridge. The magistrates, wearied of drunken behaviour, revoked its licence.

WALK 6: THE ILL BELL RIDGE

Start: *Kentmere Church. Grid Ref: 456 041*
Distance: *11¾ miles (19km), climbing 3,100 feet (945m)*
OS Map: *English Lakes 1:25,000 (South East)*
Walking Time: *7½ hours*

Here is a superb Lakeland ridge walk, including part of the classic Kentmere Horseshoe, providing a good introduction to the high fell country, with well-defined paths. The inexperienced walker should undertake the walk in settled weather. Several stretches — in particular, just north of the Garburn Pass — are boggy. On the return leg from Nan Bield Pass, becks which quickly respond to heavy rain must be forded. On summer weekends, parking is a problem, with limited space near the church. On short winter days an early start is necessary to avoid having to walk the last leg in the dark. Kentmere is reached via a minor road from Staveley, which is on the A591 between the Kendal by-pass and Windermere.

The road from Staveley to Kentmere meanders and, at first, is shaded by trees. Kentmere is in a motoring cul-de-sac, but walkers may leave the valley by way of the high passes of Garburn and Nan Bield. The 'mere' of the dale name, which a sixteenth century writer described as 'a poole a myle compasse', was reduced in size by drainage work in the 1840s. Diatomaceous earth for industrial purposes is dredged here.

Thomas Machell, a clergyman visitor of 1692, noted that Kentmere was about half a mile (0.8km) long, had a boat and 'a great store of wild duck'. Two primitive boats (possibly from the tenth century) were recovered from the bed of Kentmere in the 1950s. What appears to be the dalehead, with its rockscape and church standing jauntily on a ledge with a scattering of buildings — a hall, farms and a few houses — is only the end of part one. The valley continues to its wild beginnings, where it is shadowed by high fells. Water gathering here flows into the Kent, the main river of this segment of the Lake District.

The church is dedicated to that fine old Celtic saint, Cuthbert. This was possibly one of the halting places when the monks of Lindisfarne fled from the Danes in the

year AD 878, taking with them the incorrupt body of the saint and the head of St Oswald, a prelude to seven footloose years in the North Country before Cuthbert eventually found a resting place at Durham. A plaque in the church commemorates Bernard Gilpin, Kentmere's most famous son, who was born at the hall in 1517. Bernard, scholar and reformer, ultimately became known as 'the Apostle of the North'.

Having booted-up in the lee of the churchyard wall, stride out on tarmac, swinging left past a gate and following the signs for Troutbeck. A cottage at Kentmere has a tempting sign: 'Mugs of Tea'. The head of Kentmere is geologically mixed. An outcrop of Coniston Limestone occurs at the head of the pass but elsewhere there is flagstone, part of the great Silurian belt. In this stonescape is a huge boulder, the Badger Rock, and the walls are of special interest, being composed of large irregular pieces of rock which have become prettily decorated with grey and lime-green lichen.

Kentmere Hall (in the valley) evolved from a pele tower and was the home of the Gilpins, including the Bernard Gilpin already mentioned. Earlier, Richard Gilpin is said to have slain the last wild boar in

The buzzard is mainly a tree-nester, but was driven to inhabit remote crags because of persecution in its woodland haunts. Look for it now in wooded fellsides. This large brown bird draws attention to itself as it circles on broad wings with the flight feathers splayed upwards, uttering a cat-like mewing — peeio, peeio.

Looking towards the summit of Ill Bell on the path from Yoke, with Kentmere reservoir just visible on the bottom right. Croppers of Burneside, the owners of the reservoir, are currently making necessary repairs to it at their expense.

England. The rocky route is the celebrated Garburn Pass, a well-drained way with a gentle gradient. Among the rocks beside the pass are parsley fern and foxglove.

Garburn was part of a major drove road from the coast into Yorkshire, and a route used by jurors heading for the assizes at the county town of Appleby. It was in such a sad state in 1730 that Benjamin Browne, the magistrate at Troutbeck, ordered it to be repaired, remarking that 'it is not passable ... without danger of being bogged in the moss or lamed among the stones'. At the end of that century, William Wordsworth, his brother John and friend Coleridge, having walked from Bampton by Haweswater and Longsleddale, crossed to Kentmere, spent the night, then crossed the Garburn — on 'a rainy and raw day' — and

used the ferry across Windermere on their way to Hawkshead.

At a gate, just below the summit of Garburn Pass, bear right over boggy ground. Keep a wall to your right for the next mile, though several detours will be needed to skirt the boggiest areas. Here and there is an undisturbed carpet of sphagnum moss, which literally floats in soggy masses, having an assembly of empty, perforated cells between the cells which are living. The empty cells absorb water like a sponge, which may be easily tested. Just ring out a handful of sphagnum and see how small is the space it now occupies. Sphagnum, one of the great peat-forming plants of the Lake District, is nutrient-deficient and acid, its sterility being of use as hospital dressings during the 1914-18 war. Among

55

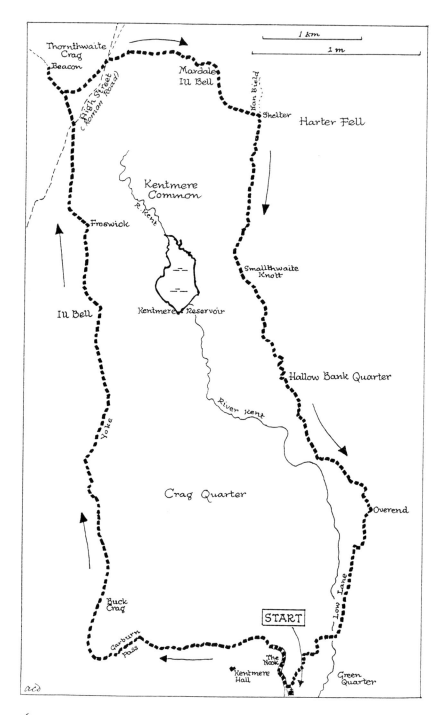

Looking back along the the Ill Bell Ridge from Thornthwaite Crag.

the plantlife in this dour landscape of peat and coarse grasses is — watercress.

As height is gained, Wansfell, over your left shoulder, is seen topping the road which struggles towards Kirkstone Pass, backed by Red Screes and active quarries. Rainsborrow Crag, the dramatic eastern face of our first mountain, may be spied (right) as height is gained. Today we will be content to view it distantly. The summit of Yoke, 2,316 feet (706m), is reached after scaling a steep wall-stile and tackling the last 300 feet (90m) of rough ascent. Do not celebrate prematurely. The first cairn marks the end of the ridge which has just been climbed, and there is another cairn set on a cheerless spot further back.

Two-thirds of a mile (1km) ahead looms the bell-like form of Ill Bell, the name being literally a hill in the shape of a bell, but the walker has to work for this eminence. The ridge dips grandly, then offers a steep but steady gradient.

The sight of Ill Bell and its small brother, Froswick, is ethereal when an east wind is whipping up a gossamer mist that sweeps up the slopes and over the ridges in tantalising waves. Ill Bell, at 2476 feet (757m), is a dramatic, airy perch, from which Froswick, 2,359 feet (720m), is seen as a mirror image, breaking up the walk to Thornthwaite Crag.

Descending again prior to climbing Froswick, the clear-weather view westwards takes in Troutbeck Tongue, the eye ranging on to Caudale Moor, near the summit of which is the grave of Mark Atkinson, onetime licensee of the Kirkstone Pass Inn.

Further north, beyond Red Screes, lie Dove Crag and Fairfield, leading the eye into the Helvellyn range. Closer to hand from the north, and swinging east, are High Street, Mardale Ill Bell, and Harter Fell and Kentmere Pike (*walk 7*). Froswick is notable as a vantage point for looking back at Ill Bell. From here it is an easy mile (1.6km) to Thornthwaite Crag, 2,569 fee (784m), which though not on the main line of the famous Kentmere Horseshoe is too handy not to be visited.

The highest part of the walk has now been reached, and you will be justified in celebrating with a snack near the cairn — possibly the tallest cairn in Lakeland and the most shapely, the fourteen feet (4m) circular pillar being visible over a vast distance. Scots Rake, the course of the Roman road linking Ambleside to Brougham via High Street, joins the course of your walk prior to the summit. A stone wall offers protection from wild weather. Entertainment is provided by the local ravens. Notice how they croak as they show off, sailing with the wind providing lift, then closing their wings to plunge for perhaps ten feet (3m) and simultaneously uttering two high notes.

Leave by a well-trodden route going north-east, initially towards High Street, the highest of the Far Eastern Fells. The path swings right at a dilapidated wall corner after one third of a mile (0.5km) and skirts Hall Cove, with its tantalising glimpses of upper Kentmere. Approached from this direction, Mardale Ill Bell at 2,496 feet (761m) is a disappointment, being best seen and ascended from Haweswater by its north ridge, which is flanked by Small Water and Blea Water respectively. The car you left several hours ago is five miles (8km) distant.

There is now a long descent, initially to Nan Bield Pass, which sports a primitive shelter at a neat col between Mardale (north) and Kentmere (south). In good

weather, you will see Blea Water, deep in its rocky basin on the Haweswater side. Before undertaking a steep descent into Kentmere, prop your back against a rock face (left) and eat up your food while watching the users of the pass — mainly walkers, moving like automata, with mincing steps, and a few visitors with mountain bikes who do their best to remain on the right side of the handlebars as they move slowly down over rock and slippery turf.

A carrion crow gives a honking sound, like that of an old-style motor horn. Crows are inclined to nest on solitary trees, their twiggy nest in the crook of branches being lined with softer material. The young are nest-bound for a long period, and when detecting the return of a parent with food, their rubbery necks straighten and their beaks open so wide they resemble a bunch of flowers.

After the early steepness, the path hugs the 1,400 feet (425m) contour on the east flank of the Kentmere Valley. The reservoir was created in the 1840s, when the mere in the lower valley, which had regulated the river, was drained and a substitute mere had to be devised. A major user of the water was the Cropper family at Burneside. The dam is no longer used as such. Several streams must be forded. One (reached immediately after using a gate) is a test of nerve and initiative. The rough track becomes a road at Overend Farm, but elect to leave the road for a waymarked path (right). Once clear of the farm buildings, stop and turn for a view of upper Kentmere.

Looking southwards again, notice that high-tension cables parallel the track. Where the cables cross, half a mile (0.5km) beyond the farm, look carefully nearby for stone steps which have been built into the walls on either side. Cross these to the right and descend to the River Kent, where there is a footbridge. A further enclosed track is quickly joined and, followed left, delivers you to Kentmere Church.

WALK 7: LONGSLEDDALE, HARTER FELL AND KENTMERE PIKE

Start: *Sadgill. Grid Ref: 483 057*
Distance: *8¼ miles (13.5km), climbing 2,200 feet (675m)*
OS Map: *English Lakes 1:25,000 (South East)*
Walking time: *5½ hours*

This is a grand walk for a good day, with a modicum of shelter as far as the summit of Gatesgarth Pass, thereafter exposed to the elements. The views, particularly those down the length of Hawes-water and Mardale, rank with the best. The ascent of Kentmere Pike is nowhere over steep ground. The descent is easy, with the exception of a few sections of rock below Shipman Knotts. Sadgill lies where the tarmac ends at the head of Longsleddale, which is a five and a half mile (9km) cul-de-sac approached via the A6 from Kendal. Leave the major road 4½ miles from Kendal at the sign for Garnett Bridge.

Longsleddale, an almost perfect Lakeland valley, was in the mind of John Cunliffe when he devised the character Postman Pat, who achieved wide fame through a television series. The valley road is narrow and winding. Drive slowly. The dale is little visited, except by walkers, for there is no through route for motor traffic. Longsleddale (like some other valleys in the fell country of south-eastern Lakeland) is a trough with steep sides composed of shales and mudstones, but across the head of the dale is the thin, persisting bed of Coniston Limestone, separating the Silurian from the showy Volcanics, the division being seen about Sadgill, where your jaunt begins.

Longsleddale has moraines (heaps left by a long-melted glacier). The River Sprint has cut a way through a terminal moraine just above Sadgill. The old glacial lake has long since drained away; its flat bed remains. In Murray's *Handbook to the English Lakes*, published early last century for the benefit of discerning tourists, Longsleddale is referred to in fulsome terms:

> *There is nothing to mar its harmony, and while passing along the narrow lanes enclosed by thickly-lichened walls, tufted with wild flowers, the eye rests on the brilliant green of the meadows …*

The situation today is not much different, despite massive changes in agriculture. Haymaking has almost been phased out in favour of silage, stored either in bulk or in black plastic bags.

Oak woodland developed centuries ago on areas of stabilised scree. Such woodland is the nesting place of the buzzard. On quieter areas of the fells, wintering red deer — the largest of the Lakeland terrestrial mammals — might be seen. The stags have had the energy-draining rut (mating season) to contend with at the onset of winter. On reaching Sadgill, take care when parking your car so as not to impede the vehicles of local farmers. Sadgill, a cluster of old buildings where your walk begins, snuggles comfortably against the sheltering west slope of Shipman Knotts, which at this level — 600 feet (180m) — is clothed in woodland.

Though now giving the impression of remoteness, Sadgill was on a route used by jurors travelling from Ambleside to the assizes at Appleby, and by droves of cattle with their attendants who were going to join the major drove route of the Eden Valley. An early eighteenth century document refers to the traffic on this 'great road and public highway' as including drovers with their

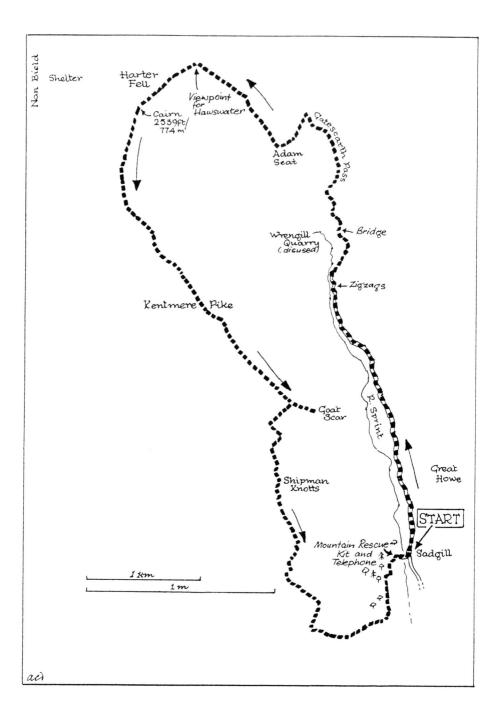

Nan Bield

Shelter

Harter
Fell

Viewpoint
for
Hawswater

Cairn
2539ft/
774 m

Adam
Seat

Gatescarth Pass

Wrengill
Quarry
(disused)

Bridge

Zigzags

Kentmere Pike

R. Sprint

Goat
Scar

Great
Howe

Shipman
Knotts

START

Mountain Rescue
Kit and
Telephone

Sadgill

1 km

1 m

aci

herds of cattle. The most irksome obstruct-ion in times of heavy rain was the crossing of 'a rivulet called Sadgill'. Sometimes, travellers had to stay at Sadgill for two or three days before they were able to cross the River Sprint with safety. The problem was solved by the building of a single-span bridge.

The first two miles (3km) of walking is at an easy gradient on the famous Gates-garth Pass, which was once good enough to take coaches, and which was greatly im-proved and somewhat re-aligned by quarry-masters. You may find yourself playing hide-and-seek with a common wren, tiny, with uptilted tail, which scurries like a mouse, but when singing has a voice of such power it can be heard across the valley. The wren has the most extensive range of any Lakeland bird in the sense that it nests in the dales and has also been found nesting on high crags, the resort of raven, buzzard or peregrine falcon.

Gatesgarth Pass ascends in zig-zags which provide for speedy walking. Drama increases on either side with every step you take. Great Howe, on the ridge above Sad-gill, boasts an unusual landmark — a survey post, not the more familiar trig point as used by surveyors of the Ordnance Survey but a much large object, with a slice taken from its centre, leaving a sighting line there-in. Another, of similar design, is to be found near the summit of Tarn Crag, further north. The posts were erected by the water engineers of Manchester who were constructing the Haweswater tunnel into Longsleddale.

The River Sprint (on your left) swirls and tumbles through deep, aquamarine pools and fully justifies the claim to be one of the fastest rivers in England, being temp-ered only when it meets the River Kent at Burneside. A series of zig-zags, stone setts on edge to increase grip, herald a steepening of your route to a gate where an ambiguous notice exhorts motorcyclists to: 'Please keep to Public Paths. No permission has

The memorial bridge at the head of Longsleddale. The plaque to Denys Beddard is just visible under the bridge.

been given otherwise.' The ambiguity comes from the fact that only bridleways on the fells may be used for such vehicles. The track beyond is indeed a bridleway, soon splitting right for Swindale, left for Mardale and Harter Fell. Before this point is reached, you will cross a bridge with an unusual memorial stone, having been set on the underside of the bridge. The memorial is to Denys Beddard (1917-1985).

To your left are the extensive Wren Gill quarries. Harter Fell may be ascended by skirting the quarries, but they are potent-ially dangerous, especially on a descent and doubly so in mist. If you are allergic to ghosts, avoid walking across Harter Fell at midnight on Midsummer Eve, when the ghostly form of a woman is on the move.

61

Take heed of the sign indicating Mardale — a sign which has in recent times received attention from the re-builders of the path. They have made a good job of it. The grass is growing back to its course. Notice during this walk the neat arrangement of four yellow petals on a small plant, tormentil, which spangles these upland areas during a flowering season which extends from June to September.

Longsleddale from Goat Scar, with Ingleborough — one of the Three Peaks of Yorkshire — on the horizon.

The view from the highest point of Gatesgarth Pass is disappointing. Here bear left, up the slope of Adam Seat, to gain a post-and-wire fence. Haweswater comes into view, the more so as height is gained. In dry periods, the receding water level leaves a white tidemark. (The west bank, remote from roads, is part of the Coast to Coast footpath.) Sections of an iron fence litter the ground and the wire acts as a snare for unwary feet. Three cairns are found in the space of 500 yards (460m) along the summit ridge. From the direction of our approach, the highest cairn, at 2,539 feet (778m) is the one furthest away, but the best views are obtained from the nearest cairn, the slope interrupting the near distance as height is gained.

The full length of Haweswater is seen at its best (*see page 3*). Long Stile, a dramatic ridge, leads from the water's edge directly to the summit of High Street which, at 2,718 feet (828m), is the highest point of the Far Eastern Fells. Long Stile is an excellent spot from which to view the sunrise over the reservoir around Midsummer's Day. The sun appears from behind Cross Fell, the highest of the Pennine fells. Wide-ranging views are had from the true summit of Harter Fell, if the weather is clear. In mist, the summit can be confusing. The north face of the fell, after an initial easy slope, becomes near-vertical. Do not venture on this under icy conditions. In the clear-weather picture to the west are Ill Bell and Froswick closer to hand (*visited on walk 6*), backed by the Coniston and Scafell ranges. The imposing Mardale Ill Bell, to the north-west, has its drama enhanced by Blea Water, which occupies a high-level corrie. Forty feet (12m) below, on the north slope, is Small Water.

Harter Fell is unusual, if not unique, in having a major pass on either side. Gatesgarth, on the eastern side, was used in our ascent. To the west lies Nan Bield, the Kentmere-Mardale route, which descends steeply into Mardale by the northern flank of Small Water. The main cairn of Harter Fell is at the fence corner. From here, follow the course of the fence southwards for 1¼ miles (2km). Near a depression, a wall takes over to lead, unerringly, to the summit of Kentmere Pike, at 2,397 feet (731m), a summit which is virtually astride the wall. A trig column (no 5636) was sited in the lee of the wall and is seen when a step-stile has been crossed. Ravens may be seen wheeling, diving or flipping on to their backs, as though using up surplus nervous energy. On our last visit, three ravens flew by at speed and in close formation, their pounding wings being neatly synchronised.

The next summit on the long descent is Shipman Knotts, at 1,926 feet (593m). A better viewpoint by far, Goat Scar, lies at the halfway point and is handy to the eastern side of the fence where it makes an abrupt right turn. Goat Scar, just touching 2,000 feet (610m), protrudes into Longsleddale, giving an excellent vista of the valley. An additional merit of the viewpoint is the velvety sward, ideal for a siesta on a warm summer's day, when it is the resort of peacock and tortoishell butterflies. You may also check from here that your vehicle is where you left it.

On the final leg, the ridge is narrow enough for a walker to descend into either Longsleddale or Kentmere from the same spot. Do not try to descend here. Windermere stretches southwards towards Morecambe Bay, which shimmers in the distance. Below Shipman Knotts, your path is never far from the wall. Care is needed over knee-cracking rocks. Remember the old adage: 'Don't walk and gawp; stand and stare.' At a cross-wall, the path linking the two valleys is met. Bear left through a gate, an easy and attractive track beside rowan trees, gradually swinging back north towards Sadgill.

WALK 8: THE OTHER BORROWDALE

Start: Low Borrow Bridge. Grid Ref 607 014
Distance: 11¼ miles (18km), climbing 1,750 feet (530m)
OS Map: English Lakes 1:25,000 (South East); the start is just off the eastern edge
Walking Time: 6 hours

For those familiar with Borrowdale near Keswick, it is a surprise to learn that another Borrowdale exists two and a half miles (4km) south of Tebay. It ends where Borrow Beck blends its water with the Lune. The northern valley of Borrowdale is alive with tourists. Its south-eastern namesake is shy, little frequented and with not so much as one ice cream van in sight. The only habitation within the little dale is Low Borrowdale Farm. This is part of Lakeland's 'empty quarter', the western extremity of Borrowdale being lost in a vast upland bloc culminating in Grey Crag, before plummeting into Longsleddale, north of Sadgill. The entrance to Borrowdale is gained from the A685 Kendal-Tebay road almost opposite the big overpasses of the M6.

Leave your transport near the first gate across the metalled road which serves the solitary farm. You are now in the Lune Gorge, where the Romans drove a road and built a fort. Nowadays, road and rail jostle each other between high fells. There are no less than four crossings of Borrow Beck, these being A685, M6, the West Coast mainline railway and a minor road connecting Tebay with the hamlet of Howgill. The creation of the motorway in recent times, after relatively peaceful centuries, was terrifying. On the first Bank Holiday weekend, when traffic was noticeably heavy, a local farmer rounding up sheep found his dog could not hear the whistle above the traffic noise wafting up the fellside.

Stay on the Borrowdale road for three-quarters of a mile (1.2km). There is a touch of mystery in the gnarled trunks of trees in a relict area of old woodland which, like many another, has no chance of survival because sheep prevent natural regeneration of the timber. Notice how many trees are rooted among rocks and swaddled by moss in an area of high rainfall. This area is pleasant for walking, but somewhat dreary from a natural history point of view, being largely acid grassland, bracken and mat grass.

Conifers planted from eight to ten years ago put on a mere three inches (1.5cm) a year.

A little after crossing a bridge which spans a minor beck, follow a rough track (sharp left) heading up the fellside. At a bifurcation, bear right, to pass through a gate in a wall and join another stretch of track heading for the skyline. The area is covered thinly by magnificent Scots pines, some of which have been toppled by gales. One old warrior, which fell on its side many years ago, has sprouted a little conifer wood of its own. The upper branches of Scots pine flake to reveal orange wood and, with the bottle-green of the needles, impart the flavour of a Scottish hill rather than a Cumbrian fell-end. This is accentuated with the first good view into Borrowdale. Framed by pines, and with a tously setting, it looks more like a glen than a dale.

You may see a buzzard circling from a distance. Notice the broad wings, curling upwards towards the tips. The call of the buzzard is a cat-like mewing. The ring ouzel, sometimes called 'mountain blackbird', is found above 1,000 feet (304m) mark. Superficially, it resembles the blackbird, but the ouzel is a summer visitor from the Atlas Mountains of North Africa. The

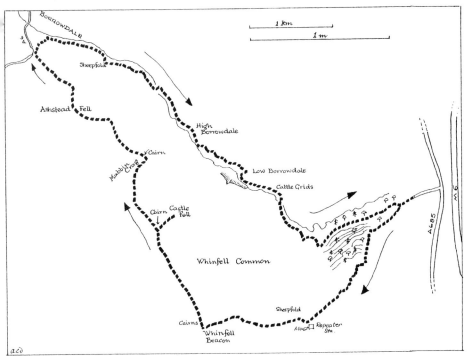

cock bird is noticeably darker than the female and so the white crescent at the chest is more pronounced. The ring ouzel has a highly nervous manner and 'chacking' call similar to the blackbird of the garden.

Pass through another gate, and the skyline is now seen to hold some space-age technology in the form of unmanned telecommunication relay stations — UGLY for short. On the left is what the imaginative might think of as a rocket for Saturn, awaiting blast-off. Our course heads for another, squatter contraption, the precourser to which led Wainwright to associate it with Martians. Extending up the hillside from Grayrigg to the south is the road used by service engineers. It has a devil-may-care fashion when intruding into the landscape.

It is not difficult to blot such towers from the mind in the glory of the fell country which lies ahead and in extensive view, taking in Kendal, the Kent Estuary, Arnside

Knott and the gleaming Morecambe Bay. Skirt a boggy area before locating a wall step-stile to the right and following a fair track which leads to a gate. Beyond the gate is a steepish gradient culminating in Whinfell Beacon, at 1,544 feet (472m). The name implies that it was one of a chain of beacons (or early relay stations!) intended to give warning or provide focal points for celebrations on great national occasions.

Undertaking this walk in a clockwise direction gives excellent views of the Coniston Fells and, closer, Ill Bell and Froswick. Descend from the summit of Whinfell Beacon to a wall junction with a step-stile, beyond which are two gates. The right-hand gate is the one for an ascent of Castle Fell, with its extensive views into little Borrowdale.

Return to the wall, which is followed from the last col and descend to another. Here begins the ascent of Mabbin Crag, at 1,580 feet (518m) the highest point on the

The A6 and Hucks Bridge from Ashstead Fell.

ridge. The Economic Forestry Group have transformed the appearance of the hill by planting conifers, as yet just a stubble. Theoretically sheep are excluded by good boundaries, but several usually manage to sneak in. The absence of heavy grazing means that plants like heather have a chance to re-establish themselves, though *Nardus stricta*, which is in cushion-like tufts, is seen everywhere. The only shelter is a stone hut, part way up the slope. A broken wall is the sole obstacle before the twin summits of Ashstead Fell are attained.

From the second summit, the view takes in the sinuous course of the A6, following the old route over Shap. The old Jungle Cafe, well-known to the drivers of heavy lorries, is now used for the sale of caravans. A steep descent from the hills leads to a point near the road (and also near the famous Leyland Clock, which now graces the Brewery Arts Centre in Kendal). The road up Hucks Brow to Shap Summit, though superseded for fast traffic by the M6, is still well-used.

The last stretch of the walk is an easy saunter down Borrowdale. Look out for the scattering of coal-black ponies on the fells. These stocky, sturdy animals are of the fell breed, which (so it has been claimed) were originally brought into the north-west to carry material when Hadrian was building his wall from Solway to Tyne. Needless to say, there is no documentary proof of this.

After crossing to the north bank, view the crumbling remains of High Borrowdale Farm. The beck's course is attended by classic oxbows. At Low Borrowdale Farm, swing right to enter the farmyard and leave on a track parallel with the clothes line. The wind can change dramatically from west to east because both ends of the valley are open. It is disconcerting, having battled with a gale for three miles (5km), only to find yourself pushing it for the last two miles (3km) back to where you have left the car, and traffic on the M6 is passing with a whine and a whoosh, creating their own form of turbulence.

WALK 9: UPDALE FROM KIRKBY LONSDALE

Start:	*the square, Kirkby Lonsdale. Grid Ref: 612 786*
Distance:	*12 miles (19km), climbing 500 feet (150m)*
OS Map:	*Pathfinder 628 (SD 67/68) Kirkby Lonsdale and Barbon*
Walking Time:	*6 hours*

Kirkby Lonsdale, named by early settlers after the church established here by the River Lune, is situated 12 miles (19.5km) from Kendal, being administered by South Lakeland Council. Most of the town, with its historic church, buildings of the native yellow limestone, squares and ginnels, is an area to be joyfully explored. It has such an outstanding situation overlooking river and dale that it was painted by Turner and became one of the favourite views of Victorian writer and art critic John Ruskin. The town stands beside the A65. There is free parking by Devils Bridge, one of the oldest crossing the Lune. Parking for which a charge is made is available a short distance away, in the square, which is usually filled with traffic early in the day and, on Thursdays, is the setting for a market, with stalls.

The square on Main Street is a nominal starting point, though Devils Bridge will do equally well, being linked to it by a tree-fringed walk. From the square, with its octagonal market cross (1905) and elegant frontage to the Royal Hotel, turn right into Main Street by the chemist's shop, passing Cats & Co and the Snooty Fox tavern. The town's air of prosperity dates back to the great days of the wool industry, when Kendal — a few miles up the road — was the main centre but Kirkby an important satellite.

In Main Street, look for a narrow ginnel, Salt Pie Lane, on the right. It gives access to an area of town which is missed by the majority of visitors. At the bottom, swing left where, in spring, the gable end of Lilac Cottage sports a gloriously flowering clematis. The narrow lane threads past half-timbered property into Haymarket. Continue across Branthwaite Brow into another square, from which a half-hidden passage leads into St Marys churchyard. The large church is plain outside, with a clock set to one side, as though the building was squinting. There is architectural glory within. Pevsner called it 'the most powerful Early Norman display'. The oldest part of the

present building, including three arches and columns on the north side of the nave, is 800 years old. Notice the diamond patterning on the columns, which is said to have been inspired by those at Durham Cathedral.

Follow the right-hand path towards a gazebo and the far-famed Ruskins View, passing on the right a precariously balanced and recently restored cottage which is maintained and leased by the Vivat Trust. Underley, the local stately home, where the Cavenidish-Bentinck family resided, is visible beyond the sweep of the river and the rich alluvial farmland, a view backed by the Middleton Fells, the resort of a few red deer, descendants of animals which had been hunted. At Underley, in late Victorian times, when Lord Bective presided, a fine herd of Shorthorn cattle was developed. The strain dated to an animal bought in Canada for the staggering sum of £9,000. Only once did his lordship sell a female from the strain. He was so uneasy about his action, he bought the animal back again.

Ruskin beheld Lunesdale from near the church and afterwards wrote:

The valley of the Lune at Kirkby Lonsdale is one of the loveliest scenes in

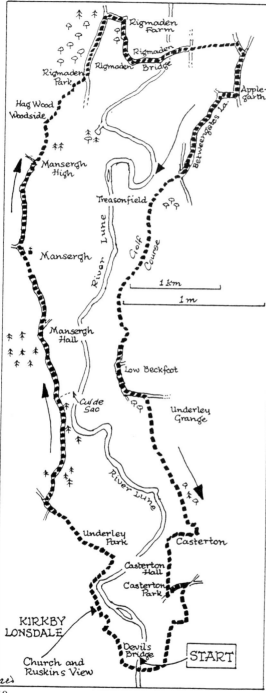

England, and therefore in the world. Whatever moorland hill and sweet river, and English forest foliage, can be at their best is gathered here and chiefly seen from the steep bank which falls to the streamside from the upper part of the town itself.

Information about this part of the bank of the Lune, known as Church Brow, is to be found on a plaque which relates that it was formerly part of the Glebelands, associated with the church, and was bought in 1947 by Alexander Pearson of Kirkby Lonsdale and given by him to the parish council, to be used for the enjoyment of the public. A collection box for money towards its upkeep is to be found close by. In the churchyard extension lies Jonty Wilson, blacksmith locally for over sixty years. He was an astonishing character, a never-dull raconteur and a man who remembered when around the old town were several large estates.

The path divides, the lower route taking a precarious course across the site of a landslip into a wooded area which, in late spring, is carpeted by bluebells and ransoms, with their strong oniony smell. Flowing to the right is a tributary of the Lune. The higher path is rejoined at a kissing-gate. Pass through the gate and follow a way-marked route, coming within easy view of what must be the largest strawberry in the world. This huge 'fruit' — for it is synthetic — is a reminder that strawberries are grown here, to be picked by the visiting public.

At the farm outbuildings, follow the tarmac way, passing a mill pond where in spring there is a gleam of

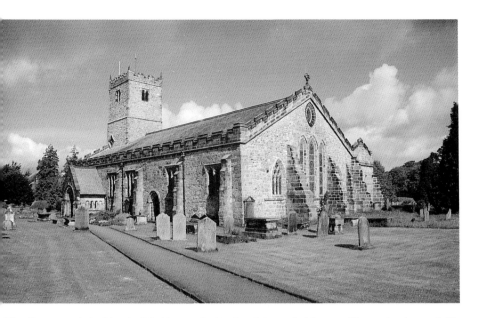

The oldest parts of the Church of St Mary at Kirkby Lonsdale are the Norman pillars and arches, probably the work of craftsmen from Durham Cathedral. Inside is a fourteenth century font originally from Killington Chapel, which was discovered being used as a drinking trough on a nearby farm!

yellow from marsh marigolds. Join the road to Old Town and follow this to the right for a short distance before opting for a minor, almost traffic-free road bound for Rigmaden and Killington. Follow this road for about a mile (1.6km), passing the gates of the long drive to Underley Hall, now a special school. Beyond Country Woodcrafts, notice a new sign indicating a bridleway to Low Beckfoot. What it does not mention is the absence of a bridge over the relatively deep and usually swift-flowing Lune. It is a short and pleasant walk to and from the riverside.

Continue for a short distance further along the road. At Mansergh Hall, an attractive farm with a backdrop composed of the big, bare, slaty Howgill Fells, bear left into a rough track. Known as Chapel Lane, it makes a bee-line for Mansergh Church. This lane is much frequented by

pickers of fruit in season. It offers raspberries, blackberries and sloes. The church, a neat Victorian structure, is open for worship on a regular monthly basis, and is one of seven churches administered by the team ministry based at St Marys, Kirkby Lonsdale.

Rejoin a road for some 200 yards (180m), passing the former school, now a private house. When the lanes make a right angle, look for a narrow track climbing away left between high and floriferous banks. The flowers include pink campion, ladies mantle and germander speedwell, the last named being short-stalked and with blue flowers, each distinguished by a white 'eye'. For half a mile (0.8km) the track climbs steadily until there is a further brief sortie with tarmac at Mansergh High Farm.

Continuing northward through a succession of gates, the route becomes less clear. Beyond a forlorn barn on the right, descend between two wooden markers to Hag Wood. Initially, and during the growy season, shorts are not recommended. The nettles grow thigh-high. The descent into Rigmaden Park is, in spring, an experience of such beauty a poet would feel frustrated using mere words (*see page 28*). The deciduous trees are well spaced. Between them are drifts of untrampled bluebells.

The path ends at a minor road which passes Rigmaden House, property of the Wilson family, one of whom used parkland to harbour various species of deer, including the sika, which is of Asiatic origin. Notice that the iron railings have verticals of extra height, so wire could be strung to form a deer-proof barrier. Rigmaden was gutted by fire but has now been splendidly restored. Turn right to descend to the River Lune. The big Victorian estate workshops have been skilfully converted into better-than-average housing.

Cross Rigmaden Bridge and follow the lane to its junction with the A683. Directly opposite, take to the fields at the sign indicating 'High Road'. A large field is crossed. The High Road has grass growing up the middle. Follow the lane right beyond Applegarth to the next junction, where a right turn leads into Betweengates Lane, in turn leading to the main dale road. Cross over and, no more than 100 yards (90m) further on, leave via a cattle grid at the sign for Treasonfield and Beckfoot farms. On the former building is a sign for 'Farm Watch', the farming equivalent of 'Neighbourhood Watch'.

Beyond Treasonfield, the track heads for a ford, with an attendant clapper bridge, the last-named being a slab of stone extending across the water. High Beckfoot Lane, a narrow bridleway, is followed for nearly a mile (1.6km). It threads Kirkby Lonsdale golf course, but golf balls are not the only hazard. Amazingly, despite is narrowness, it may legally be used by motorcyclists. It

is a pity that exhaust fumes cannot be flavoured with bluebell essence.

Beckfoot Farm sits astride the former packhorse route we have just travelled, at the point where the packhorses crossed Barbon Beck by a single-span bridge with low parapets, so that the horses' loads would not catch. Continue ahead. Scalber Lane joins on the left, passing a cluster of properties forming Low Beckfoot, before diving beneath what appears to be a railway bridge but is one built to carry a private road to Underley Hall.

Ignore a path to the Lune, continuing on Lowfields Lane, accompanied by a babbling brook. A footpath sign on the road is situated directly above a wall and raises doubts as to which side to use. Walk with the wall on your right, passing an elm tree in the last throes of a long life and climbing open ground to a step-stile. Next aim for the left-hand corner of the wood at Gildard Hill. Follow the fringe of this wood to a kissing-gate, entering coniferous woodland. A brief break is followed by yet more woodland, to the left of which is Casterton School.

Then cross a beck and swing right to enter the environs of Casterton Hall. The footpath here is in course of being re-sited, eventually leading to the front driveway. The aforementioned Casterton School was originally established at Cowan Bridge for the benefit of clergy daughters. It was attended by three Brontë girls from Haworth, and subsequently Charlotte, in her novel *Jane Eyre*, made some unflattering comments about the place, which they associated with sickness, ill-feeding and mismanagement. Yet Carus Wilson, who established the school, was not a hard man. His project was better than most. After ten years, the school was moved to its present site.

Cross the driveway to find a further kissing-gate leading to the A683, with good views of Kirkby Lonsdale to the right. Avoid further road-walking by turning left

The Devils Bridge was built around 1230 by monks who wanted a safe and permanent crossing of the Lune on the trade route between their abbeys at Furness in Cumbria and Fountains in North Yorkshire.

to follow the busy road for 200 yards (180m). Turn up a drive leading to the nine-hole course of Casterton Golf Club and follow a signposted Laitha Lane, which is yet another delightful narrow brideway evocative of the packhorse days.

At the junction, go right for Kirkby Lonsdale, soon to descend right to Devils Bridge, which is no longer used for traffic and is a gathering point for motorists and, in particular, for motorcyclists. There might be over 200 bikes parked here on a sunny Sunday. A stone bridge over the Lune was noted in 1365. The story of the Devil's involvement concerns a hand knitter of Dent who was unable to ford the river because it was in spate. The Devil offered to build a bridge, providing he received the first thing to pass over. She agreed. The stone came from the Yorkshire fells. Some fell when the devil loosed his apron-string.

On the hill is a cluster of stones, those which he had dropped. The Devil waited for his reward. The lady took a 'bannock' (a round, flat loaf) from her basket, held it to the dog, which sniffed it appreciatively. She bowled the crust across the bridge and the dog, following, was thus the first living creature to use the bridge ...

When the town had its own bank, in 1825, pound notes were issued. They were adorned by a copperplate engraving of Devils Bridge. Anglers seek trout and salmon. Sometimes, a man strides out of his depth and gets a ducking. Canon Rawnsley, Vicar of Crosthwaite and one of the founders of the National Trust, wrote:

He who goes fishing in the Lune
Without the aid of sun or moon,
Needs not a rod, but wants a stick
About his back, the lunatic!

WALK 10: ARNSIDE TO SILVERDALE

Start: *Arnside promenade. Grid Ref: 458 790*
Distance: *8 miles (13km), climbing 700 feet (210m)*
OS Map: *Pathfinder 636 (SD37/47) Grange-over-Sands*
Walking time: *6 hours*

Arnside still bears an air of Victorian gentility, several shops having glass verandahs. The dominant feature of the estuary is a fifty-one span viaduct. This walk, which is easy and has great charm and variety, takes in coastline, old coppice woodland, complete with squirrels and roe deer, and just one climb, to the summit of Arnside Knott, now planted with conifers. A nearby vantage point takes in the Kent Estuary, Whitbarrow and a range of Lakeland fells. Leave the A6 at Milnthorpe to follow the B5282 along the coast to Arnside, and park near the railway embankment where the promenade begins. Do not park on the shore. Do not venture far from the coastline. A flow tide swiftly covers mudflats and sea-washed turf.

Until 1974, Arnside was in Westmorland but with Lancashire on either side. The village was connected with Greater Westmorland by a corridor to Milnthorpe. Arnside has the feel of the seaside because of the ebb and flow of salt water in the mouth of Kent Estuary. The open bay is some way off. Arnside Knott, which has an elevation of just over 500 feet (150m), is the haunt of Scotch argus butterflies, a small, dark species which has a grassland habitat. There are only two known English colonies. A naturalist sitting in the car park by the Knott on a sunlit afternoon in summer might see the Scotch argus flutter by.

Your walk begins with a stroll along a relatively short promenade. Have a good look at the stubby pier constructed by the Lancaster & Ulverston Railway Company, which later became part of the network of the Furness Railway. The pier was needed when the railway viaduct precluded vessels from continuing to the port of Milnthorpe. An informative notice relates that the pier was rebuilt by public subscription in 1984. Make a note of the tide times from the table displayed. These are needed for later along the route. The famed Kent 'bore', at the head of a flow-tide, arrives with a rush

eclipsed only by its counterpart on the River Severn.

For the first two miles (3km), hug the coastline on the high-water mark, the haunt of fishermen who, using long rods, lots of line and multi-hooks baited with such succulent items as lobworm and slivers of mackerel, tempt a locally common flatfish known as a fluke or flounder which feeds in slack water. The average weight is from half to three-quarters of a pound (1-1.5kg), but specimens in excess of a pound (2.2kg) are not rare.

The Kent estuary is a birdwatcher's delight, with its oystercatchers (pied, with long red bills), shelduck (podgy ducks with dark heads, chestnut and white bodies), redshank (smallish, red-billed and strident) and curlew (large, streaky brown, with a long decurved bill). In winter, what appear to be dark clouds are massed waders from far northern lands. The commonest winter visitors are knot and dunlin, pale in their winter plumage. Herons are relatively common. On Meathop Moss a flock of greylag geese spends part of the winter, so a 'string' or chevron of large birds in the distance could be wild geese.

Across the bay, against a quite steep

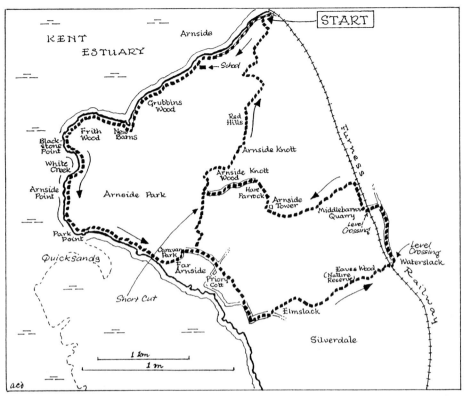

START

KENT
ESTUARY

Arnside

School

Grubbins
Wood

Red
Hills

Arnside Knott

Arnside Knott
Wood

Hare
Parrock

Arnside
Tower

Middlebarrow
Quarry

Level
Crossing

Level
Crossing
Waterslack

Furness

Railway

Black-
Stone
Point

Frith
Wood

New
Barns

White
Creek

Arnside
Point

Arneide Park

Park
Point

Quicksands

Caravan
Park

Far
Arnside

Priory
Cot

Short Cut

Eaves Wood
(Nature
Reserve)

Elmslack

Silverdale

1 km
1 m

aco

hillside, are the houses of Grange-over-Sands. Holme Island, which is tethered to the mainland, was a former home of John Wilkinson, the Victorian ironmaster who is credited with making the first iron-hulled boat and sailing it in the River Winster. Follow the concrete walkway as far as a modern coastguard station. In this area, for many years, was the workshop of the Crossfield family, builders of the Morecambe trawler, which with its sharp prow and low counter at the stern had affinities to a yacht, and was perfectly suited to working the shallow, sandy dykes of Morecambe Bay.

Grubbins Wood, which fronts the estuary, is on a limestone escarpment, the trees growing from thin soil which is acid glacial drift from Lakeland. Meadows border three sides of the wood, which is leased by the Cumbria Wildlife Trust. The wood was once coppiced, tracts being clear-felled periodically and the timber being used for a variety of wood crafts. The last cut taking place over seventy years ago. Solomons seal and lily-of-the-valley grow here, in May-June, each plant having large lance-shaped leaves, the former unstalked and the latter stalked. The white flowers of solomons seal are bell-shaped, compared with the shorter, rounded bells of lily-of-the-valley.

Grubbins Wood is rich in mosses and ferns. Harts tongue is the easiest to recognise and also the commonest, having long, broad, green fronds. The woodland rings with bird song in spring. Songs to listen for are (early in the year) the loud, ringing voice of the mistle thrush, a bigger, paler version of the song thrush, and the equally

Arnside Knott has only a modest elevation, but the view north from it is extensive, encompassing the rooftops of Arnside, the Kent Estuary crossed by the railway viaduct, Whitbarrow Scar with its distinctive limestone outcrops and, in the far distance, the Coniston group of fells.

ringing *plue-plue-plue* (or the 'yaffle') of the green woodpecker.

The first inlet along the coast tempts you to take a bee-line over the velvet turf, but this should be resisted for the channels are treacherous and, at best, you will be muddied to over your boot-tops. At the first life-buoy post, follow the line of cliffs to meet a rough track leading to New Barns caravan site. Before contouring around the headland, recall the tide times and, if in doubt, leave the shore for a short cut which rejoins

the coastal route at White Creek. Here the shoreline is partly formed of (very slippery) tide-washed limestone, complete with prominent white fossils, including crinoids.

On one visit, we had reached White Creek when we heard a siren from the direction of Arnside. It was a warning to those on the shore that the flow-tide was imminent. If you hear the siren, please take the first opportunity to gain higher ground, which is not too difficult on this shoreline. The main path from White Creek threads a (sometimes cliff-edgish) course around Arnside Point. From it, you might watch a 'sahara' of sandbar and mudbank overwhelmed by the tide. In ten minutes or so, the sea can claim its own. The first indication of the turn of the tide is usually the calls of birds displaced by the rush of water. The tidal bore passes close to Arnside Point.

On the approach to Far Arnside, descend once more to a coastline of shingle and sea-washed turf, the type of short, close, weedless turf which has been popular, when neatly cut and transported, with the owners of sports grounds or even small gardens. Look ahead to locate another life-buoy, and beyond it pass through a metal gate to cross the edge of a caravan park. A brightly-coloured and prominent bird to be seen in this area is the jay, which is actually a member of the crow family, and distinguished in flight by the white on wings and rump. The body of the bird is pinkish-brown. If you are especially close, you will notice a blue patch on each wing.

Beyond Furze Hill, you might lop three miles (5km) from the walk here described by taking a short-cut at a signpost marked 'Arnside Knott' which then passes Hollins Farm before climbing through woodland to high point near Arnside Knott. For the full walk, at a crossroads, continue ahead by path signposted 'Silverdale'. Keep a limestone wall to your right before negotiating a narrow kissing-gate. Woodland is briefly threaded before you cross yet another caravan park to join a tarmac road, the way into Silverdale. Here briefly enter the County Palatine of Lancashire. Look back, and you will see the entrance to the Leeds Children's Holiday Camp.

At Silverdale, a name with an allusion to the light tone of the local limestone, the cove has silted up (though in fairly recent times, boats from Morecambe landed goods and passengers here). It is a pretty village, the home for many years of the West Riding novelist William Riley, who made his name with his book entitled Windyridge. At the edge of town, the road swings left to Elm-slack and is lined by imposing houses.

Unknown to the majority of visitors are the back lanes which Norman Nicholson, the Cumbrian poet, compared with the secret alleys of a medieval town. One such is approached by a thin track (left) which climbs with an easy gradient to enter a snicket. Briefly join a tarmac stretch and then look for a signpost which advises 'Elm-slack, Arnside — footpath only'. It looks private but isn't, despite the bisecting of a garden, for this is Wallings Lane, which emerges on to a roadway. Go left at Castle Bank, then right for 'Eaves Wood and Witherslack'. A seat will prompt you to have a snack. Notice the well-disguised waste bin.

Continue through woodlands, skirting the rear of fine houses and passing the concrete walls of several old spring-fed reservoirs. At a bifurcation, continue ahead, passing a pair of gate-stoops made of weatherworn limestone. Ignore the path swinging left and emerge on to a garden centre car park. Cross a step-stile and yet another caravan park to see, suddenly and unexpectedly, the Carnforth-Barrow Railway. Look and listen before crossing it. On joining a quarry road, bear left. Note a sign for Challen and Hawes Water (which is a small pond, not the major reservoir). Our route passes a cottage which has been restored and stands in an immaculate garden. The road swings left to re-cross the railway and enters the huge Middlebarrow limestone quarry, where a sign indicates a path running parallel with the railway. Follow this to where the path splits, the one ahead making for Black Dyke.

The walk follows the northern fringe of Middlebarrow Wood, passing near enclosures where pheasants are bred. About half a mile (0.8km) later, the route emerges into pasture within view of Arnside Tower, one of several impregnable pele towers in which people of centuries ago took refuge when threatened by invaders. They remained here, with food and water, until those beseiging the tower grew weary and moved on. Continue past the farm to climb to a road skirting the southern slopes of Arnside Knott. The screes appear intimidating, but a gentler gradient is to be used. Pass through a gate on the opposite side of the road.

This is an old bridleway, on National Trust property, where the wildlife is profuse and rich. A sign mentions thyme, rock rose, quaking grass, fellwort, autumn ladies tresses and dark-red helliborine. The flowers and grasses in this temperate limestone area appeal to several species of butterfly, notably grayling, duke of burgundy, brown and also Scotch argus. The birds of Arnside Knott include the woodcock, which you are unlikely to see as it squats on its nest, for it is well-camouflaged against the leaf-litter, much of which is oak. Redpoll and siskin have been recorded here. Wintering birds include two Scandinavian thrushes, the fieldfare and redwing, which strip the many yew trees of their bright red berries.

As you ascend the Knott, ignore the first path to the right, continuing instead to a wall and crossing of paths (which is where the short cut mentioned rejoins the major route). Go right on the unsigned leg for the felltop. A gap in a grouping of yew and birch to the right of the path reveals Silverdale in its setting. The true summit of Arnside Knott is the trig column (S5406). The view is restricted. Walk instead to where a seat was set in memory of Councillor H B Lawson. The seat was positioned near two trees which were knotted together as saplings and grew up in this strange posture. Both are now dead. Only one trunk remains. A small boy calls it 'the giraffe'. The

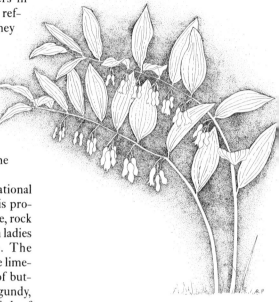

A member of the lily family, solomons seal has an angled stem, with lance-like leaves and flowers like a row of small, white, green-tipped bells

view from here is extensive, taking in the Kent Estuary and a range of Lakeland fells.

Descend south over a wall, then across a field to a wall corner, where a step-stile with hand rails allows access to Dobbshall Wood. At the road go left, then sharp right and right again at a junction. Next left will return you to the promenade, not far from where you left your car. However, finish the walk with a flourish. Look for the footpath right for the station and, following this, swing half-left into a ginnel, flanked by a stone wall and thick beech hedge. Cross a minor road into another ginnel (also known as snicket or passage). On your left is a gazebo. The path emerges close to the parish church, where you turn left. Where the road swings away left, continue on a path ahead, down to the promenade — and the full tide.

WALK 11: ALLITHWAITE AND HUMPHREY HEAD

Start:	*Allithwaite Post Office Grid Ref: 387 766*
Distance:	*4½ miles (7km), climbing 200 feet (60m)*
OS Map:	*Pathfinder 636 (SD37/47) Grange-over-Sands*
Walking Time:	*2½–3 hours*

Humphrey Head, which looks like a beached whale is, at 170 feet (52m), the highest point on the coastline between North Wales and St Bees Head, south of Whitehaven. On the headland (so 'tis said) another of the last wolves of Old England was slain. Humphrey Head, the last flourish of one of the several limestone ridges of the land north of the sands, is in part a nature reserve leased by Cumbria Wildlife Trust from Holker Estates. You may well take much longer over this short walk than is suggested. Allithwaite is a short distance to the west of Grange-over-Sands, which is reached by following the A590 from the Kendal bypass and leaving this road at a roundabout, where Grange is clearly marked. Note that the post office at Allithwaite is now in premises to the north of a triangle of roads and not as shown on the maps.

Allithwaite is named after Eilifr, a Norse settler of the eleventh century who created a *thwaite* or clearing in the woods to form a meadow. In about 1160, land was acquired by Furness Abbey. Abbot Hall was the nucleus of the present large building, a Methodist Guild holiday centre by the bay. The present village is pleasant and somewhat sprawling, being part of the limestone belt. It experienced an air raid during the Second World War when a considerable weight of high-explosive bombs and incendiaries, doubtless intended for Barrow-in-Furness, fell on the village, happily without human casualties.

Walk downhill, bearing left to pass Post Cottage to the next junction, where the Guide to the Sands Inn is prominent. This relates to the coach route on Morecambe Bay at low tide, which connected the Furness coast with Lancaster and became redundant with the coming of the railway early last century. William Burrow, who preceded the present Sands Guide, Cedric Robinson, was asked by Jessica Lofthouse, the writer, if summer was coming at last. William replied: 'This summer's bin warse nor winter — and there's warse on t' way'. He was proved to be right.

Turn right, passing an antique shop and going in the direction of Cark. The isolated house on the left has a rockery garden with models — a castle and two watermills. The castle is reminiscent of Lowther, the old home of the Lords Lonsdale near Penrith. Turn left at the Pheasant Inn, then right through a farmyard beyond. The footpath sign has lost some of its lettering but should read 'Wyke House'. The route becomes both clearer and paradoxically muddier when clear of the farm. On the hillock (left) is Kirkhead Tower, an old viewpoint, now partly ruined.

At a wooden sign, look hard (right) for a stile of the fat-man's-agony type. The level fields of a soil which has a tackiness in wet weather are part of the winter grounds of large numbers of wading birds. The silvery voices of curlew may be heard, and you will see these large waders, in their drab off-season plumage, rising at your approach. A curlew has a long neck and a long down-curved bill. The oystercatcher (also known as 'sea pie') is numerous and easy to identify, the plumage being a striking black and white and the bill long, orangey-red, resembling a stick of sealing wax.

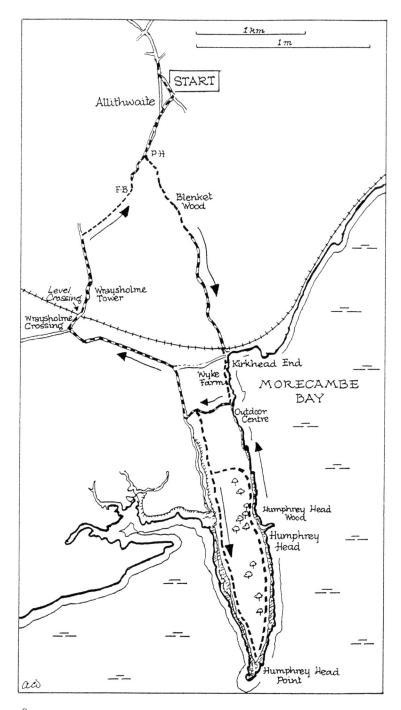

1 Km

1 m

START

Allithwaite

P.H

F.B

Blenket
Wood

Level
Crossing

Wraysholme
Tower

Wraysholme
Crossing

Kirkhead End

Wyke
Farm

MORECAMBE
BAY

Outdoor
Centre

Humphrey Head
Wood

Humphrey
Head

Humphrey Head
Point

a.d

You are now walking on the Cumbria Coastal Way, where much time and money has been spent on stiles, gates and signposts. Notice the phragmites, a reed, in the dyke (left). The trees are willows, which thrive in waterside situations. Some of these trees are of great age. Cross an accommodation road, serving an effluent works, and then use a short tunnel under the Carnforth to Barrow railway line. At Kirkhead End, go left through a gate to skirt some buildings by a marsh, where outcrops of limestone might be slippery in wet weather. The railway is seen threading its way through a spectacular limestone cutting.

Wintering geese are an attraction. They are almost certainly to be the greylag flock associated with Meathop Moss, and also found by Morecambe Bay. Geese sometimes commute to the big fields of the Lune valley near Arkholme. Shelduck, which are rather goose-like in size and manner, are locally common. The drake looks pied at a distance, but in close-up is seen to have a green-black head, chestnut body-belt and red bill.

Bear right into an enclosed track which crosses the landward fringe of Humphrey Head, to emerge where a tarmac lane serving an outdoor centre is seen beyond a cattle grid. (The public road ends at the shore, not far away, and close to a 'holy well', an obscure spring from which issues 'bracky' water which is said to have medicinal properties, being 'celebrated as a remedy for stone, gout and cutaneous diseases'.). An informative notice erected by the Cumbria Wildlife Trust reveals that you are now about to enter the Joy Ketchen Reserve, covering 55 acres (23ha). Joy was a much-respected conservation officer for the trust before succumbing to cancer in the prime of life.

Pastureland is crossed on the way to the summit of Humphrey Head. It was on this ground, in September 1992, that Sir David Attenborough, president of the then Royal

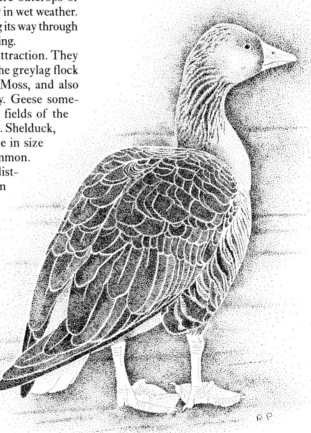

Successfully reintroduced into Lakeland as a nesting species, greylag geese can be seen in winter around Humphrey Head.

Kents Bank from Humphrey Head.

Society for Nature Conservation, accepted (on behalf of the Cumbria Wildlife Trust) the lease for Humphrey Head. The weather was wild and the proceedings took place in the swaying basket of a hot-air balloon tethered some 100 feet (30m) above the ground. For its modest elevation, the view from Humphrey Head is outstanding, the horizon being rimmed by hills, including (surprisingly, in view of the distance) Ingleborough. Westwards is Flookburgh, where a wartime airfield is now used by the North West Parachute Club, who offer tuition and the chance to jump from 2,000 feet (600m).

At Humphrey Head, the cliff edge supports red fescue and blue moorgrass, common and hoary rockrose, salad burnet (the flower heads globular and green, sometimes tinged with purple), bloody cranesbill, dropwort and the green-winged orchid. Towards the tip of the headland, which is overswept by salty air from the bay, are portland spurge (a seaside species, blue-green) and thrift (the pink-flowered plant which is present in large carpets along the side of Kent Estuary and forms cushions on Humphrey Head). A stile permits access to the limestone which outcrops on the mudflats. Keep your eye on a flow-tide.

The eastern side of Humphrey Head is less dramatic, though it is easier to gain access to the mudflats, with their wintering flocks of oystercatcher, dunlin, shelduck and pintail duck. Patches of heather are surprising in a limestone area and indicate there is a peaty covering to the rock. The woods, which are not part of the reserve, are the haunt of the red squirrel. Where the path splits, it matters little which you take, high or low, for they meet at the end of the woodland. (There is no public access to the paddock beyond.) Climb to higher ground on a path which doubles back, following a wall until a step-stile marked K3 is found.

From the other side, retrace your steps to the road which, after passing near a lime-kiln (right), swings left on to an estate road which looks as though it was planned using a ruler and a spirit level. The castellated tower is Wraysholme, once the home of the influential Sir Edgar Harrington, whose niece is said to have married Sir John de Lisle, 'a stranger wrapped in mystery', who on Humphrey Head was said to have slain the last of the free-ranging wolves. Wraysholme, for long a farm, had its tower restored some years ago. A modern hipped roof rises amid the remaining battlements.

Notice, where there are stretches of drystone wall of limestone at the roadside, that there is a profusion of harts tongue fern. At the junction, bear right to the unmanned, barrierless crossing over the former Furness Railway. Take care, for this is a busy line, carrying not only passengers but nuclear flasks bound to or from Sellafield. At a kissing-gate, which was not designed to accommodate rucksack carriers or even plumpish walkers, gain access to a field path beside a beck, which is eventually crossed by footbridge in an area where there is a pond bedecked by swan and duck. Swing to the left of Firkin Cottage to join the Flookburgh–Allithwaite road.

WALK 12: GRANGE-OVER-SANDS, CARTMEL AND HAMPSFELL

Start: *Grange railway station. Grid Ref: 412 782*
Distance: *6 miles (9.5km), climbing 1,100 feet (340m)*
OS Map: *Pathfinder 636 (SD37/47) Grange-over-Sands*
Walking Time: *5 hours, allowing for a visit to Cartmel Priory*

This relatively short walk has variety, from the ornamental park at Grange, where the free-flying waterfowl include pintail duck and barnacle goose, to the limestone pate of Hampsfell, with its hospice (a squat tower used as a vantage point) and a panoramic view which takes in Lakeland fells, Ingleborough and the estuary of the Kent, leading into Morecambe Bay. Historically, the most exciting feature is Cartmel Priory, which presides over a south-facing limestone valley drained by a watercourse with the curious name of Eea. Grange is reached via the Kendal bypass and the A590, leaving it at a prominent signpost.

The name Grange relates to a granary, or outlying farm, connected with a religious house, in this case Furness Abbey. The suffix '-over-Sands' was bestowed in Victorian times, when the place was becoming touristy. It was to distinguish the place from other Granges, and perhaps to divert attention from the muddy nature of the shore. Grange is a 'proper little sun-trap' though it faces due east. The tones of the local buildings are light, having been built of limestone.

Leaving the railway station, turn towards the town centre, passing the ornamental lake (left), which the poet Norman Nicholson described as being 'of almost excruciating prettiness'. Before the railway was built, the highest tides swept up to the main street of the village. The promenade is a good limbering-up place for walkers, and affords views of the restless tides and birdlife in profusion, especially in winter. A common local species is the shelduck, which looks as big as a goose and has a black-and-white appearance when viewed against the bright tones of the bay. It nests in rabbit holes on waste ground round the bay.

Winter is a time when vast flocks of dunlin and knot, refugees from the northlands, put on spectacular air displays, appearing from a distance like a cloud, one

moment dark, as the upperparts are revealed, and the next moment gleaming white as they turn to show the underparts. Local wildfowlers maintain a varied collection of waterfowl, some of which commute between the lake and the sands. Across the road from the park is a Victorian canopied arcade of shops (right). Take the footpath (right) to Hampsfell Road car park, climbing through woodland. Ignore the path (left) which heads for the car park and instead climb to a further bifurcation, going left to emerge onto a minor road and bearing right past Hampsfell Cottage.

In a matter of 100 yards (30m) beyond is a signpost inviting you to enter Yewbarrow Wood, where for some twenty minutes it is a matter of hide-and-seek. Sedate walkers may opt to continue on a lane which climbs steadily, swinging in a large arc via High Farm to Spring Bank, where the two routes are re-united. Woodland walkers should stay on the main track, and pass through a gate in a post-and-wire fence into what is generally known as Eden Mount. Walk carefully where there is outcropping limestone. In autumn, damp rock and leaves provide a slippery combination. Ground elder has colonised the sparse soil, and fungi is profuse on fallen timber. One

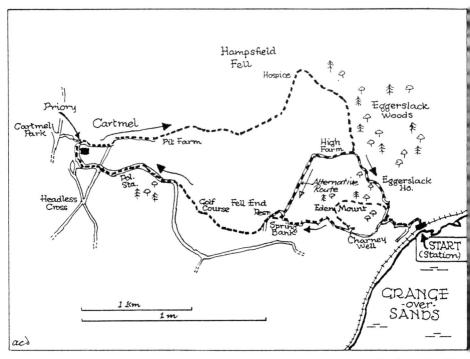

common variety, honey fungus, is known to some as 'bootlace fungus' because it grows beneath the bark and, when exposed to air, dries out in long strings not unlike the old type of bootlace.

Walk as quietly as you can in these deciduous woods, which are the haunt of roe deer. The call of a roe buck is a gruff bark. The badger also inhabits these lovely old deciduous woods, but you are unlikely to see 'our little English bear' by day. Among the many woodland birds is the great spotted woodpecker. The black plumage has white spots and blotches which enables it to blend with a sunlit wood. Notice (if there is time to study the bird) the presence or absence of a red patch at the back of the neck. Red signifies you are looking at a male bird. You may have been attracted to the bird by a rapid drumming sound — the tapping of the beak against a resonant tree branch. A screech heard in

the wood may be the call of the familiar magpie or the less familiar jay, the brightest member of the crow family, having a pinkish-brown body and a white rump which stands out against the blackness of the tail. The voice of the jay has been described as 'a raucous *skraak*'.

Keep to the main path until a T-junction is reached and the ground ahead falls steeply away. Here you should turn right and, doubling back, lose height gradually. A thin path through woodland is not far from some modern dwellings, with their trim grounds. The contrast is startling, the woodland having fine specimens of fern, notably the harts tongue, the frond being large, broad and fleshy. Emerge from the wood at a sign marked 'No tipping' and, joining a road, turn back up the hill and, eventually, right up Eden Mount, where a signpost indicates Hampsfell, via Spring-bank Farm. Palm tree and Chilean pine

Cartmel village, with the priory as centrepiece, seen from the golf course.

(monkey tree) stand incongruously side-by-side in a garden (right). The luxuriance of the local growing conditions is indicated by the way ivy has run amok, through wood and along hedge.

At the first junction, go left at an obscured sign for Hampsfell. This area of Grange, largely unknown to tourists, is a joy for walkers. In 150 yards (45m), go right again where ivy is dramatically strangling a collapsed tree bough. Now there is a high wall (left). A step-stile gives access to a pasture and, topping a rise, Springbank Farm comes into view. In the field is an impressively large disused limekiln, a reminder of the limestone terrain. Landowners and their tenants once burnt lime to be used domestically or to sweeten the grassland.

A further stile allows access to the right of a circular enclosure. Angle left round the outbuildings, leaving by metalled track which climbs to a corner where the map shows a public footpath (left). This path is unclear and, at the expense of a few yards, continue on the tarmac road, turning sharp left, where the alternative route via High Farm is met at an exhilerating viewpoint, looking out over Humphrey Head. Pass through a gate (right) marked 'No Cycling' and skirt a covered reservoir which is topped by a pagoda-like structure. Now contour the fellside through gorse, rowan and thorn. The view ranges from the sublime to the ridiculous — from Ingleborough to the twin towers of Heysham atomic power station. Ahead is the well-manicured course of the Grange Fell golf club. A stile marked 'Cartmel' leads to a footpath which crosses the course and leads you unerringly — unless you have been struck by a ball — to Cartmel village, dominated by its priory. This was built in a quiet vale between two low ridges — Bigland Heights (west) and Hampsfield Fell, now Hampsfell (right).

Do not be in a hurry if the visibility is good. Enjoy the visual treat of Dow Crag and Coniston Old Man, to the north. West, the wind turbines on Broughton Moor are a recent addition to the skyline. In the estuary of the Leven lies Chapel Island, so named (it is said) because monks from Conishead had a presence here and kept an eye on travellers who, centuries ago, took a short cut across the estuary at low tide. Aim initially for a line of trees. Thereafter the path is clearly marked to where it joins the Grange–Cartmel road. Notice that at the step-stile is an unusual variety of welly-gate (one with hinges composed of the soles of redundant wellington boots).

Taking care, walk beside the road into Cartmel village, which (as mentioned) lies in the valley of the River Eea, the name being derived from an ancient term for water. On your descent into Cartmel, notice (left) a quite large Quaker meeting house. At the T-junction, pass (if you will) the Pig and Whistle. Turn left into Cartmel on the Cumbrian Cycleway, noting at the next junction a sign which gives the mileage to Lancaster and Ulverston 'over sands', the respective distances being 15 miles (24km) and 7 miles (11km).

Cartmel has many claims to fame, notably its well-supported racecourse, in a sylvan setting to the west. Steeplechase racing takes place around the May and August Bank Holidays.

However, the most conspicuous building at Cartmel, which has the visual emphasis of an exclamation mark, is the Priory Church of St Mary and St Michael, with its curious diagonal extension to its central tower which dates to 1410. Gordon Bottomley introduced his poem *New Year's Eve 1913* with the heart-stirring words:

O, Cartmel bells ring soft tonight
And Cartmel bells ring clear,
But I lie far away tonight,
Listening with my dear …'

The old signpost at Cartmel giving the distances 'over sands' to Lancaster and Ulverston.

In the priory churchyard are sobering reminders of the old days. One family lost all five children for various reasons before any of them had reached the age of ten.

The story of Cartmel Priory began in 1190, when Willliam Marshall, Earl of Pembroke, gathered hereabouts a community of Augustinians. The twelfth century, with its border troubles, was uneasy for the canons. In 1322, the army of Robert Bruce desolated Cartmel in a sweep which also inflicted considerable damage on Holm Cultram, by the Solway, and Furness. In medieval times, Cartmel Priory maintained a guide across the Kent Sands. Edwin Waugh, the Lancashire humorist, recorded in 1882 that a traveller asked the guide if his colleagues were never lost on the sands. Replied the guide: 'I never knew any lost. There's one or two drowned now and then; but they're generally found somewhere i' th' bed when th' tide goes out.'

Curiously, the priory seems larger inside, where the white stonework includes some dog-tooth arches, than when it is viewed from out-of-doors. Light streams through a fifteenth century window which has a height of 45 feet (14m) and holds the original glass. Yet this echoing church also has its shady corners to accentuate the sense of mystery. Cartmel has cheerful volunteer guides, who will tell you about the bread charity and show you loaves of bread on a special rack. A touch of Victorian splendour is provided by the tomb of Lord Frederick Cavendish, who was murdered in Phoenix Park, Dublin, in 1882. Under one of the flagstones are the bodies of son and mother, both victims of the restless tides of Morecambe Bay, separated in death by exactly twelve months.

The priory walls are the original masonry. At the Dissolution in 1537, the roof was ripped off. Happily, part of the building (now known as the Town Choir) was preserved for local worship and in 1610 George Preston, of Holker Hall, completed the restoration and bestowed on the priory church the carved screen and pillared canopies above the old canons' stalls, which visitors now especially admire.

To resume the walk, leave the churchyard by the kissing-gate at the north-east corner, and turn right near some cottages and then left at the main road. Within yards, the next stretch of footpath will be seen, beginning (right) as an attractive flight of stone steps. The signpost indicates that Hampsfell is 1¼ miles (2km) away. Entering a pasture, follow the hedgeside (right) to Pit Farm. Pass through a gate and climb steadily on a stretch of track which is part of the much longer Cistercian Way.

To the north are seen the fells lying at the back of the village of High Newton, on the A590. Westwards may be seen the tower in the form of a lighthouse which adorns Hoad Hill above Ulverston. The 'lighthouse' commemorates Sir John Barrow (1764-1848), a native of that town who became a celebrated naval navigator. He founded the Royal Geographical Society.

The ascent of Hampsfell (the fell of a Norseman named Hamr) is initially quite steep, with bracken bestrewing the hillside. The well-defined path leads on to the limestone plateau where stands Hampsfell Hospice. The inner walls feature boards giving details of the structure. Far more interesting are the extensive views from the roof, gained by a precarious flight of outer steps. There is a large and novel view indicator. Notice, clearer to hand, the dramatic limestone clints.

Rabbits may not be popular with landowners, but they do provide a good supply of food for predators like buzzards and foxes. The brown hare may be seen. Larger than the rabbit, with black tips to the long ears, the hare spends all its life on the surface, lying up during the day in a 'form', or depression it has made in rough herbage. The 'form' takes on the shape of the body and, if a hare is flushed, may be warm to the touch. The hare is noted for its turn of speed. Its downfall in the old poaching days was that it tended to stick slavishly to certain runs. The hare is also found on rough pastureland, marshes and even woodland.

Descend towards the railway viaduct linking Grange with Arnside or, if this is not in view, go east-south-east. Waymarkers lead you to a wall corner. Keep this to your left, heading for a cross-wall with a stepstile, and joining the alternative track to the summit of Hampsfell. Continue the descent, with Eggerslack Wood on your left. Pass the first guest house. At a footpath sign, go left into the woods, taking care in damp conditions because of outcropping limestone. Keep to the high side of properties, a dilapidated cast-iron railing being your guide until, meeting a further path, you bear left to rejoin the outward route. Grange-over-Sands, long accustomed to catering for tourists, will provide you with a celebratory cup of tea.

WALK 13: WHITBARROW AND WITHERSLACK

Start: *Mill Side. Grid Ref: 452 840*
Distance: *6½ miles (10.5km), climbing 800 feet (250m)*
OS Map: *Pathfinder 627 (SD48/58)*
Walking Time: *4 hours*

Whitbarrow (White Hill) is a limestone escarpment between the valleys of Lyth and Winster, and a dominant feature beside the eastern end of the A590. The elevation is 707 feet (215m) but there is a relatively easy, zig-zag route to the top. Whitbarrow, which has the most extensive limestone 'pavement' in Lakeland, is traversed by a permissive footpath which in due course enters the Hervey Nature Reserve of 250 acres (100ha), which for a quarter of a century has been partly owned, partly leased by the Cumbrian Wildlife Trust. For this walk, take a butterfly identification book with you. Use the A590 to a minor turn-off for Mill Side and park the car beside the former highway. Parking space in nearby Mill Side is scarce.

Mill Side is one of a scattering of little-known communities in well-wooded countryside, dominated by the limestone pate of Whitbarrow. Walk into the village, passing houses with garden-proud owners. The mill dam (complete with mallard and waterhen) is adjacent to a road junction. Go right, beside a seat and telephone box. The lane splits. Take the right-hand fork, a bridleway, climbing towards Buckstone Wood. Whitbarrow Scar looms beyond. Ignore a sign (left) to Beck Head.

The mixed woodland, an amenity feature of the environs of the large Whitbarrow Lodge (private), holds larch, beech and Scots pine. All larches are deciduous. Notice, in spring and summer, that the leaves are set spirally on new shoots. They are in whorls on older wood. Beech, identifiable by its smooth, grey trunk, grows where soils are free-draining but provide it with plenty of moisture. It therefore does well in Lakeland. There is much hazel around Whitbarrow, generally forming a shrub layer rather than woodland on its own account. The male catkins open early in the year. The nuts are taken by red squirrels, which also collect monkey nuts from the bird tables of local homes.

The woods are the haunt of roe deer, a non-herding species, being also the smallest of the native deer. The buck has a short, simple, branched set of antlers and all having a pelage or coat which is greyish in winter, foxy-red in summer. The patch of light hair at the rump is shaped like a kidney. On high ground are a few red deer (named after the hue of the summer coat). If you see one, there is no mistaking the species because of its enormous size. The red deer keep the junipers well-trimmed in winter. The juniper has the widest range in the tree world, and no other species is native to each side of the Atlantic. It does not grow high and in places it hugs the ground like a tousled mat.

To the left of the bridleway (and before the Whitbarrow buildings are reached) is a small wooden sign indicating a 'permissive' footpath. This may be used by visitors through the goodwill of the landowner and not as a right.

The cuckoo pint (also known as 'lords and ladies') is distinguishable in spring by its yellow-green cowl and in summer by a cluster of bright red berries. The path ascends the scar in broad zig-zags so that nowhere is it particularly steep. The

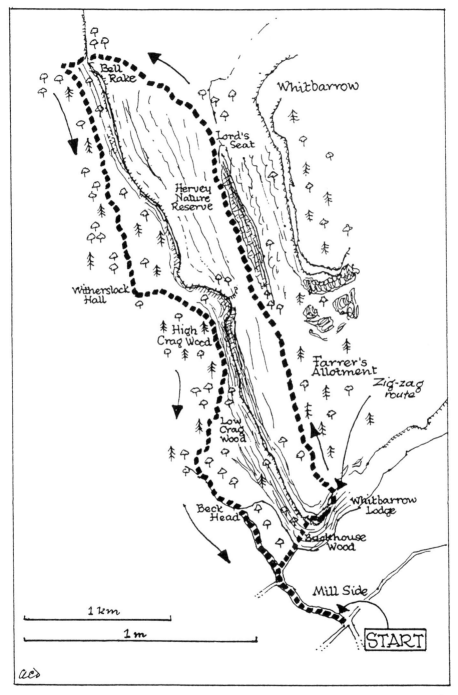

Whitbarrow

Bell
Rake

Lord's
Seat

Hervey
Nature
Reserve

Witherslock
Hall

High
Crag Wood

Farrer's
Allotment

Zig-zag
route

Low
Crag
Wood

Beck
Head

Whitbarrow
Lodge

Backhouse
Wood

Mill Side

START

1 km

1 m

aed

87

Whitbarrow Scar from Mill Side. A path zigzags through the wooded area on the side of the scar.

woodland is gloomy in summer, when the leaf canopy is present.

A wooden seat appears to view at a convenient moment, the first part of the climb being over. The view takes in Meathop Moss (much of it managed as a nature reserve by the Cumbria Wildlife Trust). The gleam of the Kent Estuary is seen and in the distance is Warton Crag, another noted nature reserve. Continue to use the zig-zag path. More hazel copse is traversed over limestone scree before the walker has to double back around a wall. The open fell lies ahead, with its birch and juniper, its ling and bracken, plus diminutive plants such as the sun-loving rock rose, spreading low on the ground, with white-woolly leaves and yellow flowers.

From the ridge, a clear-weather view takes in the Winster Valley and Cartmel Fells, with Witherslack spread among the woods below the scars. A clear path follows the undulating ridge towards the summit cairn of Whitbarrow. The mile-long walk is across or near a limestone 'pavement' consisting of weathered blocks, known as clints, the deep crevices between them being termed grykes. A gate gives access to the large nature reserve. Walkers now follow a permissive path through what is botanically the best of the area. In the grykes (take care on approaching them, for some are several feet deep) is a mini-garden of ferns and flowers. The broad, fleshy fronds of harts-tongue fern are conspicuous. Bittersweet, a small shrub with purple flowers, is best left untouched. The berries, which change from green through yellow to red, have poisonous qualities.

The summit has a neat cairn with a memorial to Canon G A K Hervey (1893-1961), the founder of the Lake District

Naturalists' Trust, which is now the Cumbria Wildlife Trust. The blue moor grass is a food plant of several species of butterfly. On a summer's day, you should see red admiral, small tortoiseshell, brimstone and small blue. The flowers which form low, deep-rooting patches on this harsh environment include wild thyme, yielding purple flowers. Limestone bedstraw, another diminutive plant, has creamy-white flowers, and salad burnet produces globular green (often purple-tinged) flower heads. The yellow flowers of horseshoe vetch are on stems which are much longer than the leaves.

Deep in the grykes lives the cowled solomons seal and also rigid buckler fern. A small tarn (a surprising feature in limestone country) is the resort of bogbean, which stands in water, has three leaflets and pink or white flowers, and also butterwort, its basal rosette consisting of leaves with sticky glands on the upper surfaces — one of nature's fly-traps. The flowers are violet in hue. The familiar cotton grass, with its cotton wool-like tuft at the head of a stem, is also at home near the tarn, being one of the great peat-forming plants.

If you are flagging, follow the cairned track, one of only two public footpaths crossing the fell, south-east to Witherslack Hall, which is about three-quarters of a mile (1.2km) away. Otherwise, use a faint track which descends north-north-west and heads for a well-maintained drystone wall, the boundary of the reserve. Birch woods give welcome shade on the hottest of days. The path runs close to a redundant mine adit; take care.

The path steepens over a limestone scree which leads to yet more hazel coppice. Beyond the western boundary wall of the reserve, yew becomes a prominent tree species. At a clearing, a new sign directs you, by permissive path, towards Witherslack Hall (not open to view), the old home of the Harringtons. In a later time, Sir Thomas

The memorial cairn on Whitbarrow Scar.

Broughton forfeited the place because he backed Lambert Simnel's rebellion in 1486. Sir Thomas lived in a local cave for some years and, when he died, was buried in the woods.

Raspberries and blackberries are abundant throughout High Park Wood. Directional arrows allow you to avoid the main tractor route. A stone shelter is seen. After a long mile (1.6km), beyond a gate stoop, a clearing is reached. It is occupied by — a football pitch. Follow the southern boundary to a step-stile, where a short cut makes its exit from the field. Cross the stile. Into view comes the near-vertical face of Whitbarrow Scar and (at the right-hand side) Chapel House Scar, which is used by climbers at certain times of year (see an informative notice board).

Continue along the main track through the wood to where a metalled track is joined near Beck Head. A stream emerges from the base of a low, much-eroded, tree-framed limestone cliff. It is an unusual and enchanting feature of a district full of surprises. Follow the lane for half a mile (0.8km). The circuit is completed when you come within sight of the dam at Mill Side.

WALK 14: BLUEBELL WOODS IN WINSTER VALLEY

Start: Cartmel Fell village hall. Grid Ref: 418 879
Distance: 8½ miles (14km), climbing 900 feet (275m)
OS Map: Pathfinder 627 (SD48/58) Milnthorpe
Walking Time: 5 hours

This Bluebell Walk, devised by the Cumbria Wildlife Trust, and one of three such walks based on the Winster Valley, has here been adapted with the trust's permission. The route is for those with spirit and a sense of adventure, being not always well marked on the ground, and with much climbing. Moments of indecision may be experienced and gates tend to be obstinate. Bluebell Week is deemed to start on the 8th May, though this depends on whether spring is early or late. Walking in the Winster Valley is pleasant at any time of the year. It's just that in early summer the sight and scent of bluebells make for undiluted joy. Small tarns add interest and variety to this most unusual walk. There is parking space near the church, in an area of trees, bird song and bracken. Try not to go on a Sunday morning, when the local churchgoers have priority, though you would be welcome to join them.

Locating the starting point from the south is by itself a minor expedition. It ends with what to many will be a joyful discovery — a historic church, tucked away in a wooded area. Leave the A590 at the roundabout some four miles (6.5km) east of Grange-over-Sands and follow the now demoted road into Lindale, turning second right past the garage and beneath a flyover carrying the A590 towards Newby Bridge. You are now in Tarn Green Lane, which should be followed due north for five miles (8km). Turn sharp left at Hodge Hill Hotel, which might easily be missed. Cartmel Fell Church and village hall, which stand some three miles (5km) east of the village of Cartmel, are signposted, second right, on an even narrower lane.

You will have time to absorb the peacefulness of St Anthonys Church (dating from 1505) in a capacious churchyard. St Anthony is the patron saint of basket makers, charcoal burners, swineherds and hermits. Here he also had to deal with the aspirations of hill farmers and their families. The present building stands on the site of an earlier place of worship, one of the survivals of which is a wooden figure of Christ of the thirteenth century. It is thought to have adorned a rood-beam and to be one of only two crucifixion figures in England which predate the Reformation. Stained glass in the east window was brought here surreptitiously from Cartmel Priory, to the south, when it was threatened by the Roundheads in the Civil War. Cartmel Fell was licensed for burial in 1712, prior to which bodies were borne to the priory ground at Cartmel itself.

Retrace your steps from the church to the hotel, noticing in springtime the cherry blossom which enlivens its grounds. Heading south on the road of approach signposted Lindale and Grange, brightness is imparted by gorse, blackthorn and primrose. The gorse usually manages to produce some blossom throughout the year. An old saying is that when gorse is not blooming, kissing it out of favour. Opposite Swallow Mire Farm, take to the footpath for Pool Bank. In the absence of a path, walk beside the left-hand wall until a footbridge is seen straddling the River Winster, one of four valleys which drain into Kent Estuary.

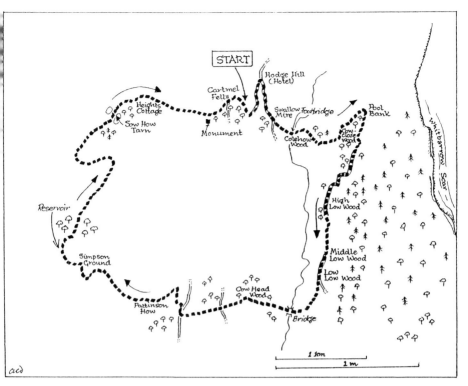

START

Hodge Hill
(Hotel)

Cartmel
Felly

Heights
Cottage

Sow How
Tarn

Swallow   Footbridge
Mire

Pool
Bank

Monument

Colehow
Wood

Cow-
close
Wood

Whitbarrow Scar

Reservoir

High
Low Wood

Simpson
Ground

Middle
Low Wood

Low
Low Wood

Pattinson
How

Cow Head
Wood

Bridge

1 km

1 m

a.w.

Swallows dart around for insect food, their twittering indicating they are feeding well. Sometimes they are in the company of house martins. Notice the white rump of the martins. The bridge is of the type which swings. If there are several members of your party, break ranks.

Turn left and cross a stile, swinging right between a fence and the remains of a wall. Whitbarrow Scar, the ridge ahead, is best known from its impressive headland, a dominating feature to the north of the A590 (*visited on walk 13*). Approaching the broken course of an old hedge, it is easy to go astray. Follow the line of the hedge to find, concealed behind a solitary bush, a further stile, which leads into a plantation in which many trees are growing in plastic 'sleeves' to protect them from browsing animals. The plantation is traversed by a thin path.

A further stile is negotiated prior to swinging left and entering Colehow Wood, where the white of stitchwort contrasts with the etheral blue-violet of the countless bluebells. A description of these familiar plants is scarcely necessary, you might imagine, but have you taken a close look at a single flower on its erect leafless stem, which holds a one-sided spike-like cluster of flowers, each the shape of a bell? Capturing the blueness on colour film is not as easy as you might imagine. These flowers are pink if taken in bright light. Choose a somewhat shaded area.

Joining a vehicular track, pass a barn to the right prior to reaching a clearing which leads into yet another bluebell wood, this being known as Cowclose. Notice a discarded millstone. The minor lane threads Pool Bank, a cluster of properties brightened by

A stretch of bluebell wood in the Winster Valley.

aubretia, yellow alysum and arabis. Turn right to follow the lane south. Ignore a sign for Witherslack, descending right to pass three farms — High, Middle and Low Low Wood farms. For a walker there is the satisfying sight of grass growing down the middle of the lane, which meanders between limestone outcrops, with cowslips to adorn its flanks. Beyond the last farm, enter a field at a sign on the right for Rakefoot, following the right-hand wall to the second of two gates as the wall descends. A path leads to a further gate where a vehicular track is joined. Go right to re-cross the Winster, a watercourse which probably has a Celtic name, as have two other rivers in southeast Lakeland, namely the Kent and Mint.

A confusing waymaker is to be found here. It is best to continue straight ahead, passing a copse of trees on the right before crossing a tributary of the Winster. Next, incline half-right to a post-and-wire fence,

crossing by step-stile. Ahead lies Cow Head Wood, bedecked by bluebells. The fragrance is strong, especially after rain. Honeysuckle climbs some of the trees. Ransoms which is generally known as wild garlic, is profuse. The early purple orchid, its flowers clustering on a short stem as stiff as a guardsman's back, helps to light up the springtime.

Emerge once more on to Tarn Green Lane, crossing this to a unstable step-stile which must be a contestant for a height record. The stile gives access to Ring Wood, which is owned by the Economic Forestry Group. Black and white striped posts were erected to warn forestry vehicles of high tension cables. Follow the left-hand track, looking carefully for a waymarker which indicates a thin path extending to the right. This path is easily missed. Climb a further ladder-stile with metal handrail — also in need of attention — and follow a path which climbs steadily through a further plastic-sleeved plantation. Gorse makes a colourful spread.

Soon a mature larch wood is entered. The purple spires of foxgloves are everywhere in summer. A squeezer-stile leads on to tarmac, where you should bear right until seeing a sign for Simpson Ground and Staveley. This track zig-zags upward to Pattison How, a ruined farm with huge cornerstones. At this point of the walk, there is a superb aspect over the estuary to Arnside. Next comes an indecisive stretch. Take a course half-right, crossing in the process the remains of two walls, while looking carefully for a lone tree standing behind a wall which is still intact. A step-stile is to be seen nearby. Beyond, the ground is boggy. Keeping the stream to your left, head for the left hand of a pair of high-tension poles. Just as you thought you were hopelessly lost, a waymarker is seen some twenty yards (15m) distant.

Follow a wall to cross the stream flanked

Blackthorn in blossom.

by calendines and marsh marigolds. At a ford, re-cross the stream and climb to Simpson Ground. At a wall corner, swing right. There is a barn on the left and a house to the right. Negotiate the gate which stands ahead and follow a sign for Staveley-in-Cartmel. Confusion is experienced at a gate bearing a North West Water notice banning admittance. It relates only to vehicles. To its right, a smaller gate indicates a bridleway as defined by the Lake District National Park authority. Ignore an early track, sharp left. When the main track forks, go right to find the dam of Simpson Ground reservoir, an unlikely spot bearing in mind the proximity of the watershed. Cowslips flower at the dam wall. Oyster-catchers are seen beside the water.

Halfway along the wall, look carefully for a waymarker into woodland. Initially there is no track, but one appears to view as conifers give way to broken ground with, on the left, the bed of a former tarn, which possibly dried out after the dam had been built. Continue north, alongside a wall. In spring the ground sparkles with the white flowers appearing from the emerald green of leaves. It is a carpet of wood sorrel. After leaving the wood at a stile, veer left where there are outcrops and meet a farm track at a wall junction. Pass through a gate and go left, still climbing, to reach Sow How Farm. The view ahead is dominated by Gummers How (*visited on walk 15*). Before reaching the farm, swing right on to a bridleway to find Sow Head Tarn, a little-known stretch of water. Coot, the white frontal disc contrasting with an otherwise dark plumage, are among the inhabitants of the tarn.

Cross the outflow stream, climbing to a waymarker by a collapsed wall. Follow the track right between two thorn trees. Boggy ground follows in woodland where a dominant shrub is the rhododendron. Several attempts might have to be made to open an awkward gate. Double back around Heights Cottage, another well-placed ruin. A nearby gate gives access to the open fell, where it is best to keep to the right-hand track on the heights heading for a well-constructed cairn about a quarter of a mile (0.4km) distant. Named simply 'Monument', it is located at the edge of a steep descent back to the Winster Valley, opposite Whitbarrow Scar. A seat is built into the structure, which is described on a metal plate as a zig-gurat, in loving memory of Martin Ruby, 1962–1993. (A ziggurat is a type of rectang-ular temple tower or tiered mound seen in ancient Mesopotamia.)

Descend the steep fellside to a wall corner, here continuing down to a way-marked stile. The track beyond leads across another wall exactly at a minor road junction, from where a footpath shortcuts back to the churchyard of Cartmel Fell. It is down all the way from the church.

WALK 15: GUMMERS HOW

Start: *Gummers How car park. Grid Ref 390 877*
Distance: *1 mile (1.5km), climbing 400 feet (120m)*
OS Map: *Pathfinder 626 (SD28/38) Broughton in Furness and Newby Bridge*
Walking Time: *1 hour*

Gummers How is a commanding hill at the southern end of Windermere. This walk is the shortest in the book, being included because of its deserved popularity. It provides great views for a modicum of effort. The starting point is reached by following the A590 from the Kendal bypass, turning right for three-quarters of a mile on the A592 from Newby Bridge. You climb steeply (still in your vehicle) for a similar distance by Fell Foot Brow, which is the high road bound for Kendal. The commodious Gummers How car park is on the right.

In the days when steamers operated on Windermere (they were converted into diesel craft), one of the sailors was patrolling the deck when he saw a visitor looking sorrowfully over the side. He explained that a watch, a family heirloom, had slipped from his hand and was now lost in the lake. The sailor told him not to worry. 'Give me half-a-crown, and when we clean the lake out at the back-end of the year, I'll get it back for you.' The visitor remarked: 'I don't believe you clean out this lake.' Said the

The ascent of Gummers How is easy, but offers ample reward to the most casual of walkers.

Gummers How, easily attained and outstanding as a viewpoint for Windermere and the Silurian fells.

sailor: 'Of course we do — and over there [Gummers How] is where we put all t' muck'.

A geologist would find another explanation for the existence of the How, one of the grand vantage points of Lakeland in the area of Silurian rocks. Gummers How, composed of a hard gritstone, stands out in a landscape which suffered greater erosion. The antiquarian William Stukeley, impressed by the local hills, and aware of the considerable rainfall, imagined 'the vast solidity of the stone that composed them attracts the clouds big with water at some considerable distance, and then the winds break and dash them into rain'.

Having parked your car, in an area beside a road which is now quiet but once was busy with traffic avoiding the marshy ways nearer Morecambe Bay, walk a short distance further north to where a kissing-gate (left) gives access to a clear track which has recently been 'stepped' in places. The path will lead you without difficulty to the summit. Initially, there is thin tree cover,

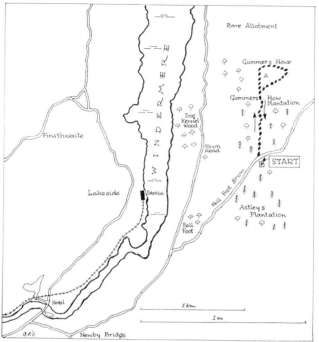

potential and authorised its extension to the side of Windermere, where railway company steamers carried the Victorian tourists to Bowness and Waterhead. To transport one of the smaller craft, the rails were lifted in a tunnel and it was single-tracked for a short time while the unusual cargo was inched through. The double track was then replaced.

When, on your ascent of Gummers How, the summit is not far away, there is a choice of routes — a steeper, left climb or one which continues to the right, following a fence, and curving to the left for the final stretch to where the summit is marked by a well-masoned cairn. Preferably use this right-hand route for the descent. Go to the summit in late summer and you will see a purple tinge where the heather has flowered. The summit view takes in the whole of Windermere, which is ten and a-half miles (17km) long, though only about half a mile (0.8km) wide.

A visitor to the How was heard to recall reading Arthur Ransome's book *Swallows and Amazons* (set in this area) and to remark that the view reminded him of the book's endpaper map. The view takes in Esthwaite Water, a relatively shallow lake near Hawkshead. In the south-west, the lighthouse-memorial to Sir John Barrow, a native of the area who achieved high office in the Admiralty, is prominent on Hoad Hill, above Ulverston.

Return to the car park by the path you followed on the outward journey.

with some silver birch and lots of geriatric larch, trees which sprang up when the eighteenth century planting had its day. Indeed, this might almost be a repository of larch which have reached pensionable age. Each is a character, twisted and gnarled. One or two, having withstood high winds for many years, are so bent they are almost touching their toes.

During the ascent of Gummers How, some of the most interesting features of Windermere's western shore come into view. They include the Lakeside jetty of the Windermere Iron and Steamboat Company, where the majority of the fleet of old but wonderfully-maintained craft are berthed overnight. A steam train service operates from Haverthwaite to Lakeside at prescribed times. Originally, this line was a branch of the Furness Railway from Ulverston and served the ironworks at Backbarrow. The railway directors became aware of its tourist

WALK 16: DOWN DAMSON DENE

Start: *Lyth Valley Hotel. Grid Ref: 453 896*
Distance: *3½ miles (5.5km), climbing 200 feet (60m)*
OS Map: *Pathfinder 627 (SD48/58) Milnthorpe*
Walking Time: *2 hours*

This short but much varied walk is at its most memorable when the snow-white damson blossom is at its peak of beauty, in late April or early May. The orchards are situated in limestone country. The blackthorn's blossom gives the well-trimmed hedgerows some eye-catching white patches. There is much of interest at this western edge of the valley whatever the season and, of course, in a good year the damsons themselves are ripe (and being offered for sale locally) in the autumn. To reach Damson Country, take the A590, opting for the A5074 at Gilpin Bridge. The Lyth Valley Hotel is three miles (5km) north of the junction, with a layby opposite, on the left of the road.

What is generally referred to as the Lyth Valley should really be Gilpin Valley, after the river which rises to the east of Bowness. The much-improved road through the Lyth Valley is signposted as for Bowness. Lyth (from the Old Norse *hlith*) means a hillside. Which hill was in mind — Scout Scar or Whitbarrow? Each would make a worthy contestant. During the walk, you might see a notice relating to the landowners of 'Cros-thwaite and Lyth' on the flanks of Whitbarrow.

The name Lyth Valley is associated in the popular mind with damsons. A Victorian novelist, Mrs Humphry Ward, described the Lyth Valley in spring-time in her book *Helbeck of Bannisdale*:

The course of the bright twisting stream was dimmed here and there by mists of fruit blossom. For the damson trees were all out, patterning the valleys; marking the bounds of orchard and field, of stream and road ...

A recent poet, Margaret Cropper from Burneside, wrote:
The damson's abloom, it blows so slight,
Like a young lamb in a spring dawn.'

So it is today, though on a smaller scale since when Lyth Valley damsons were in keen demand by visitors and were sold in large quantities in Kendal market. There is also the gold of daffodils and, in summer,

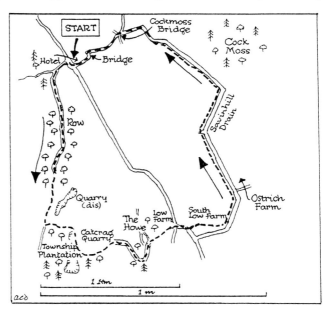

hedges ankle-deep in meadow cranesbill, a misty blue.

From the north end of the layby, a bridle-way climbs between moss-covered lime-stone walls. Ferns, ramsons (commonly known as 'wild garlic') and dog violet ab-ound. Branches of damson trees from an adjacent orchard extend over the wall. The path splits. Go left, passing an attractive property on the way to the Row, a straggle of white or grey houses in a grey and white limestone setting.

In spring and summer, the gardens are as colourful as pictures on a seed packet. The damson blossom has a del-icate fragrance as well as being showy. Daffodils and narcissi abound. On gar-den walls are sheets of aubretia and arabis. Fringing the lane are grape hyacinth and honesty. Where the route becomes tarmac-ed, bear left, noting almost immediately a footpath sign opposite. At Fairview, double back right into what quickly becomes an enclosed way flanked by hawthorn. The path heads for woodland. Look out for a stile over wire to the right. (A footpath sign would be helpful here.)

Now under a leafy canopy, with celan-dines peeping through the grass in early spring, bear left at open ground, with a cross-wall on your right. Enter and cross a further orchard which has a springtime display of naturalised daffodils and prim-roses. A new stile, half-left, leads into copp-iced woodland. Struggle through the foll-owing squeeze-stile to take the right-hand track through an area of limestone clints and grykes. The slots, or foot marks, of roe deer might be seen on the path and, in quiet circumstances, the deer themselves may be seen as they move off behind a screen of yew trees. The roe is a relatively small deer, greyish in winter, foxy-red in summer, with a white rump–patch the shape of a kidney.

The path is joined by another from the right. Almost at once, a crossroads is

Damson blossom can be seen in May. The ripe fruit is on sale in September.

encountered. Opposite, the sign of a badg-er's paw-mark indicates the route bound for Whitbarrow and the Hervey Reserve of the Cumbria Wildlife Trust. The badger's paw is the trust emblem.

Go left, following a vehicular way which was used when a large number of small quarries were being stripped of their lime-stone. Thankfully this activity has stopped, and the Cumbria Wildlife Trust are spear-heading a campaign to protect the compar-atively few limestone pavements which remain. The majority are to be found in Cumbria and North Yorkshire. The path goes near what appears to be an abandoned millstone, except that this thick circular piece of limestone with a hole at the middle is an impressive six feet six inches (2m) in diameter. Cowslips thrive in this area.

Ignore branches left and right to emerge from woodland and descend to a metalled road at a T-junction. Turn left here and look for Low Howe, where a narrow lane descends to meet one even narrower. Look for a footpath sign and a squeeze-stile, immediately followed by a more convent-ional model. Keep the hedge to your left and emerge on to the A5074 at Low Farm.

You are advised to cross the road directly to South Low Farm rather than risking a crossing of the road where it forms a bend. Join the signposted path beyond the bends on your left. Here the character of this walk changes dramatically and, were it not for Scout Scar in the middle distance, you would be excused for thinking you were in the Fens or even the Somerset Levels.

Margot Adamson, in a poem about the Whitbarrow area in spring, referred to Lyth as a 'wide silent valley'. Once the tides swept the area between Underbarrow and Whitbarrow, but natural silting and man's eagerness to reclaim the wetlands artific-ially have curbed the flow and ebb of the sea. The Lyth Valley is patterned by drains. The once-wild little River Gilpin is now embanked. In recent years, the much-improved road from Levens to Barrow has destroyed the character of the lower valley.

The path you follow extends along the top of a flood bank, to where three step-stiles in succession negotiate fencing where cattle habitually drink in the river. Meeting a minor road, cross the bridge which spans two watercourses, the lower system being pumped into the higher, the River Gilpin, which in its soundproofed bed is another reminder of Fenland. Where the road makes an acute right turn, you may find yourself rubbing your eyes several times and finally convincing yourself that there are some captive ostriches. Forsake the road and continue ahead along an unmetalled

A spectacle of springtime flowers in the Lyth Valley.

track, at the next bifurcation veering right to walk beside a watercourse with the dole-ful title of Savinhill Drain, which is bridged at several points. The valley is not one of unrelieved green, as it appears at first glance. In the tracts least capable of being cultivated are clumps of wildness — moss, tufty grass, with a scattering of birch trees to give the place a Scottish flavour. Red deer have harboured in these rarely visited places.

The real Lakeland is now in view. Clear-ly visible to the west are Bowfell and Crinkle Crags, at the head of Great Langdale. The virtually level track swings left to Cockmoss Bridge, where five lanes meet. Enter the narrow one opposite, walking with a lime-stone wall on one side and a quickset hedge on the other.

A modest climb over a hillock makes a welcome change from the level ground. The descent is beside a damson orchard adjacent to the River Gilpin, which here is bridged. The river has its guardian mute swan. The hotel, where bar snacks are avail-able, has a dining room with an impressive view of the valley.

WALK 17: WEST OF WINSTER

Start:	*Winster village hall. Grid Ref: 417 936*
Distance:	*4½ miles (7km), climbing 400 feet (120m)*
OS Map:	*English Lakes 1:25,000 (South East)*
Walking Time:	*2½ hours*

When Central Lakeland is bursting at the seams, go over the hill to Winster for a walk in relative peace and quietness, through attractive but unspectacular countryside, visiting an unsuspected tarn and, from Rosthwaite, having a surprise view of Windermere, with a horizon crowned by the Langdale Pikes and other shapely fells. Use the A5074 (Gilpin Bridge to Bowness). There is space opposite the village hall in Winster for three or four cars.

Winster, a scattered hamlet, is at the head of a quiet valley which runs parallel with the south-eastern side of Windermere. It is not normally thought of as walking country, and tends to be 'clarty', with sticky mud, but has its rewards — a whiff of old estates, quiet woods and copses, carpeted by bluebells, and a ragged stretch of common with view of blue-remembered fells. The River Winster, a little-known watercourse, rises on the southern slopes of Undermillbeck Common, flows almost due south for twelve miles (19km) and is stung by the salt water of the Kent Estuary near Lindale. The name Winster may refer to 'white', but no one is sure about this. More certain is its old-time importance. Until 1974, when the Boundary Commission played fast and loose with our borders, the river was the boundary between Lancashire North of the Sands and Westmorland.

From where you have parked the car, cross the road, having first listened for approaching fast traffic on a blind corner. Note the sign for Birket Houses. Stride out initially on tarmac, passing Mid Winster House. A descent opens up a sylvan view, with High House Farm prominent. Many of the old farms of Lakeland have whitewashed outer walls which gleam against the verdant green. Where circular chimneys were built, this may not have been just a matter of style but the best way to use random pieces of stone for building.

A step-stile at the edge of woodland gives access to farmland which, at the time of our visit, had just been ploughed and re-seeded. Few old meadows, with their herby mixture, remain, the need being for lush grass which grows quickly and may be mown in May to be ensiled as winter fodder for the stock. Note the tractor wheel which fills a gap in a drystone wall. The next sign indicates a diagonal course across a field. Presumably, the farmer would prefer you to follow the edge.

Gain a clear track once more at Birket Houses, where drystone walls have been constructed using the old Cumbrian skills on a new stretch of boundary wall for an estate of some 3,000 acres (1,215ha). This and an older wall are of outstanding quality. A drystone wall is really two walls in one, each bound to the other by large stones known as 'throughs', with small stones to fill in the gap and a row of capstones to turn the weather and make the wall look attractive. Extra appeal is given to the Lakeland walls by mosses, which grow freely and well in the damp, unpolluted air, and ferns of many kinds.

A well-made drive, with flanking open drains and substantial boundary walls leads to Winster House, with its capacious outbuildings, doubtless built to house coaches

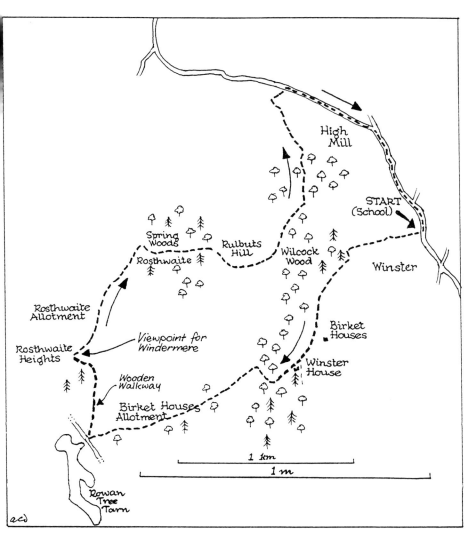

and horses. Swing right before the house and continue the climb with a steepish gradient, passing a line of beeches so close together they probably started out life as a hedge. The beech thrives on soils which are freely drained, even acid soils. It demands a great deal of water. The crown of the tree is such that while the beech may grow under other trees, none will find satisfactory conditions under a beech.

Emerge by gate onto a rough road, leaving this immediately as indicated half-left by a ground marker. The Coniston range is now in view across undulating country. Further north are Crinkle Crags, Bowfell and Pike o' Stickle. While crossing Birket Houses Allotment, and prior to arriving at Ghyll Head Road, you will see a tarn due south. Arriving at the road, cross it to see Rowan Tree Tarn, its waters held by an inconspicuous dam. The rowan, after which this stretch of water is named, is everywhere apparent, and in late summer is speckled with clusters of vermilion berries, attractive to ring ouzels, soon to migrate to the Atlas Mountains of North Africa, and also to redwings and fieldfares, refugees from the Scandinavian winter.

A backdrop to a view of the tarn is wooded Great Tower Plantation, owned by the Boy Scout Association. The moored objects on the tarn make a noise to scare off cormorants, coastal birds which, with sea fish scarce, are visiting inland waters to feed. These large birds could soon strip a tarn of its best fish.

Recross the road, choosing one of two paths. Each heads for Rosthwaite, the right-hand path crossing boggy ground on what appear to be old railway sleepers. The left-hand path uses access land negotiated by the National Park authority. The paths rejoin near Rosthwaite Heights where, by a solitary tree, a further path forms a T-junction. Continue due west for a short distance and, at a cairn, you will find yourself on a vantage point for Windermere. Looking north, the head of the lake leads the eye into the great hollow flanked by the Fairfield Horseshoe. The eye, swinging right, takes in Red Screes and Caudale Moor, the Ill Bell Ridge and, finally, Tarn Crag and Grey Crag, overlooking Longsleddale.

Retrace steps to the T-junction, here turning left for Rosthwaite. Those familiar

The ring ouzel or 'mountain blackbird' resembles the familiar garden bird, but has a whitish edging to its feathers and a white 'bib', the male being noticeably darker overall than the female. They tend to nest in craggy, upland areas of Lakeland, migrating to the Atlas Mountains in North Africa during the winter. The cool, clear notes of the cock ouzel's song indicate the coming of spring.

Rowan Tree Tarn among the quiet hills between Winster and Windermere. Beyond the water is Great Tower, a famous camping area of the Boy Scout movement.

with its Borrowdale counterpart will be disappointed to learn there is no shop with ice cream and cold drinks. Here, where stood an old Lakeland farm, is a splendid house, a traditional barn much restored and other outbuildings relating to the owner's love for equestrian activity. An exercise yard is deep in tree bark. A motorised capstan-like device is for exercising horses. An enlarged pond is home to a variety of water-fowl — and a plastic heron.

A sign for Winster indicates a climb, right, through Spring Wood to Rulbuts Hill. The view is so extensive there is a glimpse, far to the east, of Ingleborough, a bulwark of Yorkshire. Descend on a clear track through an area of gorse. The track is joined by another one. Wilcock Wood is encountered to the south of High House

Farm. The track into the farm complex is private but a track on either side of the gate ahead returns you to the A5074. The right-hand track is quicker, the left drier.

Joining the road, bear right to return to your car. *En route*, you will pass Compston House (c1660), which not so long ago, when it was a post office, was one of the most photographed buildings in the land. Sheets of aubretia drape the garden walls. Inside, in the old days, was a wall clock with a shrapnel hole in its face, inflicted, so we were told, during the London blitz some fifty years earlier.

Standing alone on a minor road opposite the Brown Horse Inn is Holy Trinity Church, built in 1875 of stone quarried locally and here at Winster having an almost perfect setting.

WALK 18: CROOK TO STARNTHWAITE

Start :	*Crook. Grid Ref: 462 951*
Distance:	*6½ miles (10.5km), climbing 750 feet (230m)*
OS Map:	*English Lakes 1:25,000 (South East)*
Walking Time:	*4½ hours*

This route is off-the-well-beaten track. In several places, the route is less apparent than the map would have you believe. A ruined church is visited in the back o' beyond, a former school is a little closer to civilisation, and a tarn, clearly shown as such on the map, virtually disappears in a drought. The starting point at the scattered village of Crook is two miles (3km) from the junction with the northern end of the Kendal bypass of the B5284. Locate the second turn to the left after passing the Sun Inn (which is on the right). There is limited parking beside the road.

Pass a former mill complex which is now a residential area with names still associated with the old mill. It was at Crook, in the eighteenth century, that the first bobbin-making machinery was developed by John Braithwaite of Ellerbeck Mill. Soon there were bobbin mills throughout South Lakeland supplying the textile industry. The road from Crook climbs steadily to a T-junction. A footpath sign (across the road) directs you over a stile. A further stile announces 'Agricultural land. Footpath only', a euphemism, for in summer the bracken is almost as high as the eye of the proverbial elephant.

Bracken, once extensively mown in autumn and sledded or carted to the farms to provide bedding for stock, is now unwanted and has spread rapidly. The plant, which has rapidly colonised old pastures, standing up to six feet (2m) high, and shows its not unattractive fronds. The plant extends its range by means of underground rhizomes. By late summer, the foxglove, which flourishes in Lakeland, stands like a spent rocket. This tall herb, best known to us in a woodland or hedgerow setting, had livened up the early summer with its spire of purple flowers. A few plants flower well into the summer.

You are now entering an area of gentle gradients, with mossy stones, little woods and buzzards, which give mewing calls, as though some cats had become airborne. Big and brown, with rounded wings, the buzzard — a bird which tries not to exert itself — circles on the thermals. It nests high in deciduous trees and eats a variety of food, from sheep carrion to the dor beetles which infest sheep droppings. Having been exterminated in this area by game interests in the nineteenth century, the buzzard was re-colonising its old woodland haunts in this part of Lakeland in the 1930s and is now relatively common.

The thickets of gorse, dense and spiny, soon reveal who has set off wearing shorts. The yellow flowers brighten up the spring and the shrub gives excellent nesting cover for small birds, such as linnets. In the wooded areas, a parrot-like squawk — *skaaak, skaaak* — or a sound like the tearing of a stiff calico-like material signifies there is a jay in residence. This highly-coloured member of the crow family is recognisable in flight by the blue and white patches on its wings, and a white rump. You may see little more before it hides itself away in the foliage. In autumn, it can be seen feeding on acorns on the ground where there are open, park-like conditions.

Climb to a gated wall stile, beyond which the path (barely discernible) swings left.

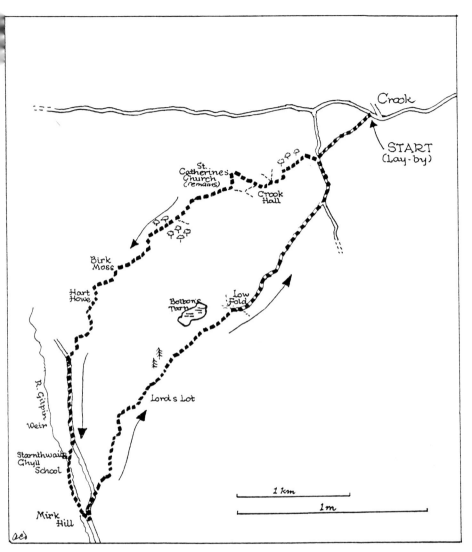

Overhead power cables act as a guide to the route. Head for a cross-wall, following its course round a corner (left) looking for a further stile backed by a small copse, the trees growing from between mossy boulders. The copse shelters Crook Hall Farm, where there is a 'sphagetti junction' of paths, five in all. With the farm buildings to your left, pass through a gate near to a power cable pole, promptly leaving by the next gate on the right.

Ahead lies a clover-clad track, decked in summer with harebells, which have a delicate stem and subtle shade of blue. The track ascends to a walled enclosure which defends a lofty tower, of the early seventeenth century, all that remains of St Catherine's Church, which served Crook parish

The now-ruined tower of the former Church of St Catherine, in use for nearly 400 years until the end of the last century.

between 1516 and 1887. This church site seems remote but was on the Pilgrim Way from Kendal to Furness Abbey, avoiding swampy ground. Then, because of structural defects, the body of the church was demolished. The tower was restored in 1993 with the aid of grants from English Heritage and the Lake District Special Planning Board, plus a donation in memory of Judy Logan (1963–1989) of Birk Moss. To the rear of the enclosure is a cripple-'oil (a creep-hole allowing sheep to move

between pastures). The new church can just be made out in a shelter-belt of trees due north. A wall from the old church, dated 1470, and bearing the coats of arms of both England and France, was moved stone by stone to the present church.

Retrace your steps from the old church tower, and follow a wall (left) to a step-stile from where the main track is clearly seen, some fifty yards (45m) away. Rejoin it and bear right. A ruined wall shortly provides company. The wall is lined with blackthorn, hawthorn, honeysuckle and bracken. Hawthorn was once a much-prized tree, being the plant which gave its name to the thickset hedge, a real barrier to farm stock. The thorn takes a long time to grow but has a long life, hence its value to those who produce wooden objects in a turnery.

Pass through a gate. A stream is bridged. Beyond, to the right, stands Brow Head Farm, framed by the Langdale Pikes. From a wood on the left a further path extends from Low Fold, which will be seen on the return leg. On a metalled track, turn left to cross a cattle grid, signed 'Birk Moss', then right, the zig-zag being repeated, though without a cattle grid. The farm complex of Birk Moss, home of the Judy Logan who was commemorated at the old church tower, is avoided by a clearly-marked diversion. You now join a track from High House at right angles on the ridge of Hart Howe, a good viewpoint in good weather for Bryan Houses Plantation, which is backed by Great Tower Plantation, a celebrated camping area of the Boy Scout movement. Westwards are the Coniston Fells, and to the south the valley hems in the River Gilpin, which is bound for Sampool Bridge and its confluence with the Kent. The huge block of masonry on the horizon is the power station at Heysham.

A good track descends the hill, between thickets of gorse. In a pasture over a wall you might see some pot-bellied ponies.

Himalayan (or Indian) balsam grows tall and stout-stemmed, putting forth big pinkish-purple (sometimes white) flowers between July and October. Its seeds are dispersed on hot summer days, the seed pods drying out and then springing open at the slightest touch, hence the plant's alternate name of 'jumping jack'.

107

Passing through a gate, leave by the next gate (left) beneath an overhanging bough. The track is now less clear, but head towards a farm complex with a blue-tinged roof, to emerge on a minor road. Go left on this quiet byway as far as Starnthwaite Ghyll, which was formerly an approved school in a glorious setting and is now a set of flats for some fortunate families. A bridleway skirts the left of the buildings, leaving via a gate in the boundary railings, where a faded sign indicates 'Right of way is restricted to Footpath'. Within a short distance, a further gate gives access to a road and bridge over the River Gilpin, a watercourse named after an old Westmorland family.

The banks of the river are floriferous, a dominant plant in summer being a hardy immigrant, Himalayan balsam, which here is rampant. At the road junction, by turning left, opt for Starnthwaite and Crook, quickly leaving (right) on the public footpath to Low Fold, climbing steadily under a canopy of trees. An arrow at a gate points indecisively left.

The map shows a clear path, but on the ground there is little sign of disturbance. Take heart. Head north-north-east, looking for a fence to your right and a stream (left). Here a stile gives access into something less than the Promised land. A mini-jungle of bracken gives way to a man-high expanse of prickly gorse, through which the path weaves a sinuous course. You will see a wall (left) and soon reach Lords Lot, a plateau. Make a detour (right), passing a stone carved with the initials R H and the date 1811. This leads to Nigh Hill, from which there is a good viewpoint for this undulating, well-wooded landscape.

Back on your main route, you might like to add Boltons Tarn to your list. The tarn, hidden by a low, grassy ridge, is little more than a reedy pool. Low Fold, which was mentioned on the outward leg, is soon passed. It is followed by High Leys, tucked away betwen hillocks. On the metalled track, a spanking pace returns you to the public highway where, turning left, you will complete the circuit within minutes. Bear right for the B5284 and the Sun Inn.

WALK 19: EAST OF BOWNESS

Start: Bowness, the Glebe. Grid Ref: 398 965
Distance: 7½ miles (12km), climbing 1,200 feet (370m)
OS Map: English Lakes 1:25,000 (South East)
Walking time: 4 hours

Bowness, which has all the trappings of tourism, seems an unlikely starting point for a fell walk. However, behind the town — and away from the lake — lies a fairy-tale landscape which is bypassed by the multitudes of trippers to the lakeshore or to the higher fells beyond. This walk explores an area of mini-peaks, mini-valleys and enchanting woods. Minor eminences offer classic views. Travellers to Bowness from the south should follow the Kendal bypass to the terminating roundabout and turn left, motoring along the B5284 via Crook.

At the end of the seventeenth century, Celia Fiennes, who was among the first of the 'curious travellers' to Lakeland, travelled on horseback from Kendal to Bowness. The road was too narrow for a carriage. She was anxious to see the lake, having heard of a fish called char which, in its potted form, was said to have a delicate flavour. One of the authors, when he was a small boy, visited Bowness in the company of two maiden aunts, travelling by rail by way of Lakeside, thence by steamer to Bowness, returning home from Windermere station. (For him, the highlight was not potted char, but ham, eggs and crinkly chips at the Arcade Café.)

Bowness is Blackpool-ish in the high

Bowness and Windermere, with the Langdale Pikes on the horizon (left).

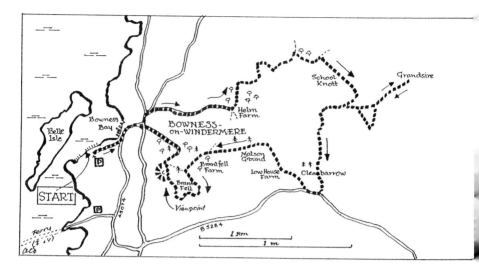

season. Arthur Ransome, who wrote adventure stories with Lakeland settings, called this touristy place by the lake 'Rio'. Harriet Martineau, who in the mid-nineteenth century wrote the most stimulating of local guides, described Bowness as 'the port of Windermere', adding grandly: 'There the new steamboats put up; and thence go forth the greater number of fishing and pleasure boats which adorn the lake.'

It is a place you cannot ignore. And on a sunny day, when the waves slap their feet on a shingly beach, when the white boats come and go, and waterfowl in vast numbers clamour for food, it can be exciting. The view northwards across the lake extends to the craggy fells of the Volcanic series of rocks, notably Fairfield, brooding her horseshoe retinue of fells. Bowness is not the easiest (or cheapest) place in which to park a car, so an early arrival is recommended. Walk to Bowness proper along the waterfront, looking up the lake to the 'jaws' of the Fairfield Horseshoe.

The waterfowl, already referred to, are varied as well as numerous. The coot is instantly recognisable because of its dark plumage and white frontal disc to the head

— hence the expression 'as bald as a coot'. The mute swan, largest of the birds, can be ferocious in defence of its nest but at Bowness it waddles among the crowds. The squabbling mallard, some of which bear witness to having been crossed with domestic strains of duck, accept tit-bits of food from the hand. The most common gull is the black-headed, which has a dark brown 'hood' in summer and loses it in the moult and in winter simply has a dark mark behind each eye. This gull has a raucous voice.

William Wordsworth, in *The Waggoner*, mentions the owls which frequented the woods beside the lake just south of Belle Isle, when the ferryboat was a modest craft, propelled by oars. A traveller might have to hail the ferryman if he was across the water:

Upon the banks of Windermere
Where a tribe of them [the owls]
*   makes merry,*
Mocking the man that keeps the ferry.

The Belsfield Hotel (see a large wall-top notice flanking the promenade) was built in 1848 for the Countess de Sternberg, and subsequently purchased and enlarged by the Furness industrialist, H W Schneider. There are extensive grounds.

Walk through the centre of the town and continue right up Crag Brow, where the shops were constructed in the 1860s. An immense chestnut tree which stood at the brow was felled in a road-widening scheme. Turn right again into Helm Road, passing the Cats Whiskers (left) and Crag Brow Cottage (right). Beyond lies the Hydro Hotel, once grandly known as the Windermere Hydropathic Hotel, dating from 1881, a time when those with means and leisure and sluggish livers 'took the waters'. The hotel of today looks down on Bowness Bay.

Where the climb steepens, take a signed path (left) at the edge of an oak wood and above the road. The path leads to a viewpoint on Biskey Howe. Those visitors in wheelchairs can conveniently approach the viewpoint from the road immediately beyond it. An outcrop of Silurian rocks at a forty-five degree angle is a challenge to the adventurous. In Victorian times, ladies were impeded by their billowing clothes but, at Biskey Howe, steps were cut in living rock for their benefit. (Some of the paths you will traverse date back to Victorian times and have good gradients and, where necessary, steps.) The slate view-indicator on Biskey Howe dates from the queen's silver jubilee of 1977 and encompasses a vast panorama, from Bowfell to Ill Bell. Raspberries and black-berries are to be picked in season. Ensure you pick only from above the safety level — say, two feet (0.6m) — this being a favourite dog-walking area.

Descend eastwards to rejoin the tarmac at a road junction and continue in the same direction. Within yards there are signposts to help you find your direction. Still walking on tarmac, head for 'The Helm'. At the first bifurcation, go left (cul-de-sac) and at the second, veer right, ascending beneath

The coot, a squat water-bird which is slaty-black with a white frontal disc, builds a twiggy, waterside nest in secluded areas round Windermere.

trees. Soon a further path is encountered at right angles. Go left here through a kissing-gate and follow a course between rock outcrops, not far from high-quality housing. Cross a step-stile, turning right by a well-trimmed hedge of *Cupressus leylandii*, which ensures privacy for the property-owners beyond. At the Bowness equivalent of Spaghetti junction, take the path half-right. It is denoted by the figure of a dog on a disc (no fouling) and a footpath sign for Windermere.

Now you will cross gardens, quite legally, to emerge by the Norweb Lickbarrow substation. Turn left near a neglected kissing-gate and, reaching a minor road, go right, ascending with an open grassy space with public seats (left). From here, the view takes in part of suburban Bowness, Windermere (river-like, with well-wooded banks) and, beyond the gently rolling Silurian countryside, the craggy peaks of the Volcanics, including the Coniston Fells. The road eventually flanks a field in which there is a redundant bath, turquoise in colour, now serving as a water tank for cattle. Immediately opposite is a step-stile, which should be crossed. In view over the wall to your right is School Knott. The path is intermittent, descending to a stile, followed by a bridge and an attractive flight of slate steps, ascending to a road which looks private but is open to walkers. To the left stands Old Droomer, flanked by plants and with a well-manicured garden just across the road.

Through the gate beyond is a new sign for School Knott. Now you have really shaken off Bowness. The moderate climb leads to an elevation of 760 feet (233m) and to a viewpoint for a wide range of fells, with the Langdale Pikes occupying centre stage. Not many birds stir in this area. A skylark rises from tousled grassland and somehow finds the energy to maintain station, high in the air, and produce a cascade of silvery

notes. The meadow pipit, one of those 'little brown jobs', has some white feathers in the tail. The song flight is something special, the bird descending with stiffened wings and tail, giving it the appearance of a shuttlecock. The pipit tries to infuse some life into the area but does not achieve much (except with another meadow pipit) with its simple *see-er, see-er*.

Descend to School Knott Tarn, which invites you to settle down to eat or nap. Follow the wall on your left to the first gate, which gives access to an upland pasture. A series of solitary trees (which is not a contradiction) leads to the rugged summit of Grandsire, at 818 feet (251m). The view takes in the fells around Kentmere and also the Howgills, smooth and wall-less, which someone compared with a herd of elephants that had lain down to rest. Retrace your steps to the trees to swing south over a bridleway, the Dales Way (Ilkley–Bowness), and ascend to the fourth viewpoint of the day — an unnamed outcrop of rocks, from which there is a splendid view southwards to Morecambe Bay.

The landscape has been well nibbled by sheep, but growing from cracks in the rocks are remnants of the old herbage — two heathers (bell and ling), bilberry, juniper, holly, rowan. The last-named, which is also known as mountain ash, is a native tree which has the distinction of growing at a higher elevation than any other and yet is common in suburban streets. The vermilion berries, which are ripe in late summer, provide a feast for birds, especially ring ouzels, building up their strength for the return flight to the Atlas Mountains of North Africa.

Retrace your steps to the gate, veering left to the Dales Way, bound for Bowness. The track meanders through an area patchy with gorse and crosses Scout Beck, before taking to grass to join a clearer track (left) and recrossing the same beck. You are now walking due south on an enclosed lane, passing through a series of gates, to Clea-barrow. Beyond lies a minor road (B5284) which carries fast traffic. Turn right and hurry for some 200 yards (195m) before recovering your composure from the flurry of traffic and errant golf balls, for the Windermere Golf Club is close at hand.

Swing off right by a postbox at Low Cleabarrow. A yellow arrow gives reassurance. Blackberries are in plentiful supply. Look for a sign 'FP Dales Way' and here turn left, locating another yellow arrow on a telegraph pole. Cross a stile to where damson trees overhang the path. The damson does well in this part of Lakeland, a celebrated area being the Lyth Valley, where in a good flowering season for damson trees, parts of the valley give the impression they have been covered by a light shower of snow.

Your course is now punctuated by kissing gates. The terrain bears the marks of glaciation, and near Matson Ground is a tract of flat ground which was once the bed of a lake. This formed when the area had been scooped out by ice. Matson Ground, an imposing range of private buildings, has a name dating back to the time when parts of the old common were enclosed. There are several 'grounds', each taking its name from the original owners. In the early part of the sixteenth century, what became Matson Ground was the setting for an iron-smelter.

A minor road is crossed near Matson Ground. Where the path splits, go left beneath a stand of ash, emerging to cross tarmac and to walk beside railings (left). The Langdale Pikes are again in view. Beyond Brantfell Farm, steps are encountered at the start of the approach to the last great viewpoint of the day. Brant Fell, another of the Silurian foothills you are visiting, has an elevation of 629 feet (193m). The path is 'permissive' (used by special permission from the landowner) beyond an enclosure wall. The summit of Brant Fell has striking rock outcrops. Look around and you will find the foundations and gates stoops associated with a former summerhouse.

In view are the lower reaches of the lake. W G Collingwood observed that Windermere is not one lake, but two at least, 'joined by narrow channels at the group of islands which nearly cut the two great basins apart.' You will see the Round House on Belle Isle (restored after a serious fire). The ferry operating south of Bowness looks no larger than a water-beetle. The Langdales crown the north-western horizon. Descend left (ignoring the route used in the ascent of the fell) and negotiate a step-stile. A track beyond climbs to a small rock outcrop, Post Knott, before joining a clear path through woodland. It is a path well used over many years, as evidenced by several stone slab seats. Where the Dales Way crosses, turn left, passing a stone tablet on a gate stoop. The associated flag seat is 'for those who walk the Dales Way' to Ilkley.

The path joins Brantfell Road, which leads directly to Bowness. At Belle Isle View is a further tablet (right) relating to Apple-thwaite and Undermillock School, which was founded in 1637. The plaque is from the school house which was erected by John Bolton, of Storrs, in 1836. He wished 'to promote in connection with the Church of England the temporal and eternal interests of the population of these hamlets.' Colonel Bolton, who lived at Storrs Hall, south of Bowness, died in 1837, and therefore just missed the opening of the school he had endowed. Imagine his feeling today if he could return and emerge (as you will do) into the press of people and traffic opposite St Martins Church, Bowness.

If you dare cross the road where there are no traffic lights, have a quiet spell in church, where (wrote W G Collingwood) 'there is one beautiful heirloom of antiquity left, the east window ... originally in Cartmel Priory ... and though restored, so well restored that there is no cause to complain.'

WALK 20: ORREST HEAD FROM WINDERMERE

Start: Windermere Railway Station. Grid Ref: 413 987
Distance: 2 miles (3km), climbing 400 feet (120m)
OS Map: English Lakes 1:25,000 (South East)
Walking Time: 1¼ hours

Alfred Wainwright, the daddy of all fellwalkers, made his enduring acquaintance with the Lake District at Orrest Head, which is owned by the National Trust. A plan to erect a monument to Wainwright on the summit of this fell did not get through the planning stage. Not that Wainwright would have worried. A simple memorial to him is set on a window ledge in Buttermere Church, facing out over Haystacks, where his ashes were scattered. The Orrest Head walk is frequently done in shoes or high heels with equanimity, if not equilibrium. The return is often made by the same route. Options are shown and reflected in the distance given. Park the car in a roadside space (A591) on the Staveley side of the Windermere Hotel.

If you do seek parking in Windermere town, you will have to negotiate a one-way traffic system. There are two catering places in the vicinity of the railway station. Now cross the A591 to the pavement beside the Windermere Hotel, an enormous building which was built to accommodate the increasing numbers of wealthy tourists who visited the district after reading guidebooks, or seeing paintings and engravings of the natural wonders of Lakeland. Until the coming of the railway in 1847, the area in which you start this walk was known as Applethwaite (Windermere was adopted by the railway company and rapidly expanded into a town). Applethwaite Common extended up the side of Orrest Head until the enclosures of 1831.

To the left of the Windermere Hotel is a large sign marked Orrest Head. Initially, the route is on tarmac, climbing steadily in sharp loops, beneath rhododendrons, introduced from alpine areas of the Far East and extensively planted in the grounds of large houses in the heady period which followed the arrival of the railway. Also in view is the laurel, another evergreen and a favourite of our grandparents, though it was first brought from its native Mediterranean

haunts in the sixteenth century. Ignore a path to the left, which is used on the return.

The woods, once the exclusive haunt of red squirrel, are now mainly within the

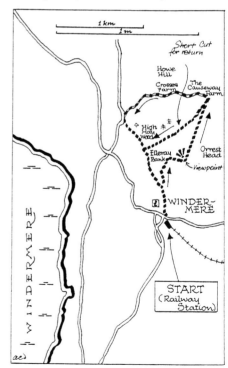

territory of the thrustful grey squirrel. The sound like ripping fabric is the call of a jay which, if you see one, is seen to be the mostly brightly coloured of the crow family. If a deer is seen, it is almost certainly the roe, which is relatively small as deer go, has a small, simply branched type of antler, dark marks which look like a moustache and, if seen departing, a light rump patch the shape of a kidney. The voice of an alarmed roe buck is a coarse bark.

The route leads to Elleray where, in May 1811, Professor John Wilson (a friend of the best-known people of the time and a man who wrote sensitively under the pen-name Christopher North) led the former Miss Jane Penny, now his 'bright and beauteous bride', on their honeymoon. He thought, as Wainwright was to think in modern times, that there is no such another prospect in all England than that from Orrest Head. The professor, a great character, enjoyed robust activity. He indulged in Cumberland and Westmorland wrestling, and was also a keen freshwater sailor, to whom regatta day on Windermere was a highlight of the year. He once flung himself out of a boat in mid-lake, as though taken by a bad fit, and pretended he could not swim. Domestically, he enlarged the southern end of Elleray as a drawing room. Before the flooring was put in place, he organised here a 'main' of cock-fighting, a sport long since outlawed.

The tarmac ends at Elleray Wood Cottage. Close by, at a bench opposite some

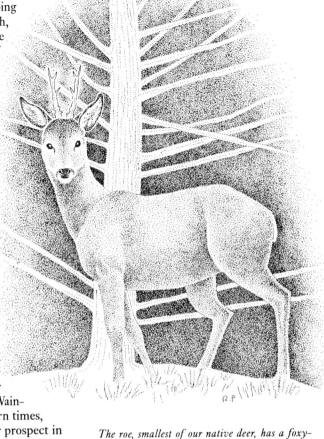

The roe, smallest of our native deer, has a foxy-red coat in summer and is greyer in winter. The buck (pictured) carries small, pronged antlers. The best time to see roe deer is at first light, as they graze in quiet fields near their woodland habitats.

dual-wheeled gates, go right. Anyone in high heels will find the going marginally rougher beyond, though there is no danger of going astray. Seats are provided where there is a high stone wall. Gaps in woodland give views over the lower reaches of Windermere — the lake, that is. A large brown bird circling on broad, rounded wings is a buzzard, which nests in woodland and feeds largely on small mammals. Occasionally, one of Lakeland's few golden eagles might be seen soaring above the district, having slipped over from its usual haunts around Riggindale and Haweswater.

At a break in the wall is a kissing-gate, bounded by stone tablets. That on the left commemorates the family of Arthur Henry Heywood who, in his memory, dedicated Orrest Head to the public in perpetuity in 1902. That on the right has family words from Keble:

Thou who has given me eyes to see
And loved this sight so fair
Give me a heart to find out thee
And read Thee everywhere.

A short climb through an area of bracken and coarse grasses leads to the summit, with its memorial seats and viewfinder. Now before you, in clear weather, lies the 'promised land' — a view across the rolling Silurian landscape. The hills first claim the attention. Then Windermere, the largest lake in England, is scanned. Despite its cubic capacity, Windermere is long and compact; the shoreline has lots of wooded knotts which impinge on the area to be viewed.

From Orrest Head, you can see the sudden transition from the somewhat gentle Silurian country, around Windermere, to the knobbly fells of the Borrowdale Volcanics, immediately to the north. The flanking hills are detailed on the indicator, which rests on a stone plinth. Look in particular for the Old Man, presiding over the Coniston group of fells. Two of the guardians of the head of Langdale — Pike o' Blisco and Crinkle Crags — are clear to see and, in exceptionally clear weather, you might view Scafell Pike, the 'attic' of England. The indicator reveals the direction of the Fairfield group and, almost due north, High Street, while to the east the view extends into Yorkshire, with flat topped Ingleborough (one of the celebrated Three Peaks of Craven) easy to identify.

When should you go to Orrest Head?

The simple answer is: when the horizons are sharp and you can see a breath-taking panorama. W G Collingwood, the Lakeland historian, in his charming book *The Lake Counties* (1902) wrote: 'On a clear summer evening it is best; or when the snow is half-way down the hills, and the woods are a brown glow in the level winter sunshine.' It was Collingwood's opinion that a battle was fought on Orrest Head and that the name 'Orrest' is a late Anglo-Saxon word derived from the Norse word for 'battle'.

The widespread view from Orrest which was seen and enthusiastically described by Wainwright on his first Lakeland visit in 1930, when he was twenty-three years old. He recalled, in *Ex-Fellwanderer* (1987): 'I saw mountain ranges, one after another, the nearer starkly etched, those beyond fading into the blue distance. Rich woodlands, emerald pastures and the shimmering waters of the lake below added to a pageant of loveliness...' Orrest Head is in its grandeur out of all proportion to the modest elevation of 785 feet (239m). It was the start of his love affair with Lakeland. In due course, he obtained a job with the borough council at Kendal, the town which became his springboard to paradise.

The first of what he called 'pictorial guides', and dealing with the Eastern Fells, was revolutionary, being reproduced entirely as he presented it to the printer — handwritten, with meticulous drawings and maps *in situ*. All the printer had to do was to make blocks from the pages. Wainwright, a very private man, yet managed to imprint his humour and personality on the minds of millions of readers. And it was on Orrest Head that a new way of looking at landscape had its origins.

The wearers of sandals and high heels should return to Windermere using the line taken on the ascent. Others, more suitably shod, may continue northward, descending with a wall to the left. Notice how the rough

Alfred Wainwright, 1907–1991.

vegetation is succeeded, on the lower slopes, by good pasture. In the eighteenth century, the whole of Orrest Head was under cultivation, as noted by the topographer Thomas West. He mentioned small enclosures.

Ahead is limewashed Causeway Farm, an old farm which is high-tec now, with milking parlour and slurry tank. Before the farm is reached, there is a step-stile in the wall to be used and, beyond, an indistinct path which contours the shoulder of the fell, joining a tractor-way which heads for High How Wood (right). Incidentally, you have crossed the Thirlmere–Manchester aqueduct, traces of which are now slight.

Ignore a gate into the wood, opting instead for the thin track which follows the wall (right). Cross a further step-stile and, at a spoil heap, swing left over rising

ground. Aim for a point where the wall to your left meets another which flanks the woodland ahead. Pass through a gateway and over a stile to have the direction confirmed by a yellow arrow — the waymark. The track, embowered by trees, is enclosed by walls. At a junction, bear left to emerge shortly on the route of the ascent. You are only fifty yards (40m) from the A591.

A longer option, adding an extra half mile (0.8km) is to continue to Causeway Farm and follow the minor lane left, descending this to its junction with the A592. Leave immediately through a gate to your left (signposted 'Orrest Head'), initially on a metalled track over open ground. Across a bridge lies a tract of woodland, in which you might see the nuthatch or a treecreeper, small, brownish, with a thin decurved bill, which settles at the base of a tree, then advances upwards, pausing to pry with its bill into cracks and crannies where insects or grubs (items of food for the bird) may be lurking. In winter, a treecreeper is sometimes seen in the company of a flock of assorted titmice, birds of a family which includes in Lakeland the great, cole and blue tits.

The track, which is foolproof, threads to the rear of impressive houses, with high walls/fencing to their gardens. Briefly, cross a private road to traverse an enjoyable stretch of terrace. At North Point, continue ahead between it and a garage to join the shorter route of return which comes in on your left. Continue ahead for the A591, rejoicing that the path has not been taken into a road-widening scheme. (Earlier, it had been intended to take the railway through from Windermere, previously known as Birthwaite, to Ambleside.)

SELECTED READING

General
Brian Paul Hindle, *Roads and Trackways of the Lake District* (Moorland, 1984). History and development of the road network.
Tim Locke (ed), *The Holiday Which? Guide to the Lake District* (Hodder and Stoughton, 1989). Practical, well-informed and always stimulating.

Literature
Grevel Lindop, *A Literary Guide to the Lake District* (Chatto & Windus, 1993). An exhaustive study of writers, poets and their work relating to local locations.
David McCracken, *Wordsworth and the Lake District* (Oxford, 1984). A guide to the poems and their places.

Natural History
G A K Hervey and J A G Barnes (eds), *Natural History of the Lake District* (Frederick Warne, 1970). A team of naturalists deal with Lakeland geology, plants, insects, fish, birds and mammals of the various habitats.
Jim Taylor Page, *A Field Guide to the Lake District* (Dalesman, 1984). A mass of information in easily available form. Copiously illustrated.

Topography
Michael Ffinch, *Kendal and the Kent Valley* (Hale, 1983). Popular history and tradition.
Norman Nicholson, *Greater Lakeland* (Hale, 1969; republished). Includes Kendal and Morecambe Bay.
Christopher D Taylor, *Portrait of Windermere* (Hale, 1983). Geology and social and economic influences, presented in an easily understood and most interesting way.

INDEX

Illustrations are numbered in *italics*